# BERLIN

A VISUAL AND HISTORICAL DOCUMENTATION
FROM 1925 TO THE PRESENT

MARK R. McGEE

# BERLIN

## A VISUAL AND HISTORICAL DOCUMENTATION FROM 1925 TO THE PRESENT

THE OVERLOOK PRESS
WOODSTOCK & NEW YORK

This edition first published in the United States in 2002 by
The Overlook Press, Peter Mayer Publishers, Inc.
Woodstock & New York
Woodstock:
  One Overlook Drive
  Woodstock, NY 12498
[for individual orders, bulk and special sales, contact our Woodstock office]

New York:
  141 Wooster Street
  New York, NY 10012

Editor: Antje Heer, Berlin
Recent photographs: Jonas Maron, Berlin
Book design by: Pauline Schimmelpenninck, Munich
Typeset by: Mega-Satz-Service, Berlin
Printed by: H. Heenemann, Berlin
Bound by: Lüderitz & Bauer, Berlin
Printed in Germany

Library of Congress Cataloging-in-Publication Data
McGee, Mark R., 1960-
  Berlin : A visual and historical documentation from 1925 to
  the present / Mark R. McGee.
    p.cm.
  1. Berlin (Germany)—Buildings, structures, etc. 2. Berlin
  (Germany)—History—1918-1945. 3. Berlin (Germany)—History—1945-1990. I. Title.
DD891 .M34 2001
943'.155087–dc21
2001036051
9 8 7 6 5 4 3 2 1
ISBN 1-58567-213-0

*Baroque palace on the south side
of Pariser Platz, 1865*

# CONTENTS

# FOREWORD

*Wolf Jobst Siedler*

"Von diesen Städten wird bleiben: der durch sie hindurchging, der Wind!"
(What will remain of these cities is what passed through them, the wind!)
When Brecht wrote this line of verse in the twenties, those who read it
probably understood it as a poetic metaphor for the transitory nature of
modern civilisation. Europe's cities were firmly established and it seemed
unlikely that one day all that would pass through them would be the wind.
But a major quake must have been in the air. Georg Heym wrote his
famous lines on an impending war before the start of World War I and
Fritz von Unruh said at the beginning of the thirties that, if Hitler were
to seize power, he could imagine "sheep grazing on Potsdamer Platz."
This became reality only a decade later. When fighting stopped following
a further world war, sheep were indeed grazing in the Tiergarten and the
wind was blowing through gutted walls.

Perusal of the photographs in this book brings home the apocalyptic
visions of these poets. The Berlin of our parents and grandparents indeed
no longer exists. Nothing makes this more apparent than to walk through
the streets and squares of Berlin. Of course, Paris and London have also
changed radically, the society which existed at the turn of the last century
on the Seine and the Thames no longer exists. But the buildings where
Balzac and Maupassant lived are still there, and it is still possible to
ascend the narrow flight of steps which led to the imaginative salon of
the Duchess of Guermantes. In London too, the districts where Dickens
and Thackeray once lived have remained intact and the Kensington and
Knightsbridge of the nineteenth century are still standing at the beginning
of the twenty-first century. Indeed, a guide to literature could serve as a
map of the city: only very few of the places described in works of literature are no longer there.

But where in Berlin is the wine tavern frequented by E.T.A. Hoffmann,
where is the Potsdamer Strasse known to Theodor Fontane, where did

Alfred Döblin have his medical practice for the poor, and where is the bar where Gottfried Benn "had a quick beer" as he used to say in his letters and poems? Gone with the wind, not only because the air raids and street fighting reduced much of old Berlin to rubble. The immediate post-war generation dreamt of a brave new world, which was to be reinvented in its entirety. The "urban landscape" of Scharoun was to replace the "sea of stone" of Zille and Mehring. At the time there were huge bill-boards on which the city proudly announced its intention of practising tabula rasa on a grand scale: "demolition for reconstruction."

Since then half a century has passed, and Berlin has made every ef-fort to restore the city. Where the smoke-blackened ruins of houses once stood, today only very few empty lots are left as a reminder that these were once the site of something else. The city is in the process of be-coming a normal major European city, even if it has to remain an open question whether today's Berlin can again be called a metropolis or may-be even a cosmopolitan city. Much is still lacking and probably it is not so much the buildings as the people who are missing. The saying that Berlin is a cosmopolitan city without any cosmopolitan inhabitants did not arise by chance.

But perhaps this is what has always distinguished Berlin from other European capitals, which in the case of Rome go back thousands and in the case of London and Paris hundreds of years. Berlin is, seen in this context, a very young city and this is still very clearly reflected in its ap-pearance. It is not so long ago that it was an electoral city and even when it became a royal city in 1701 it had under 100,000 inhabitants. However, after that things happened quickly. By the mid-nineteenth century, Berlin had a population approaching the one-million mark and from then on it grew at a furious pace. Towards the end of the Bismarck era, the popula-tion of Berlin increased every two years by the same number which it had had at the time of Frederick the Great. To exaggerate, it could be said that Berlin is a city without any history of its own which has a historical role to play. So why should this not be reflected in its buildings?

A perusal of the unusually interesting photographs in Mark McGee's book brings to mind the famous saying that Berlin never is, but is always in the process of becoming. To take the example of the Gendarmenmarkt, probably the most important square still remaining from old Berlin. The quadrangular square is still dominated by Schinkel's playhouse flanked by the two cathedrals designed by Gontard, which Frederick the Great had built in the last years of his life. Yet today it is very difficult to imagine the proportions of this square when standing at the foot of the Schiller monument in front of the steps of the former playhouse.

The theatre and the two cathedral buildings once dominated the site, which was bounded by two-storey Baroque houses. During the Bieder-meier period one or two additional storeys were added to these buildings.

*Above: Belle-Alliance-Platz with the Peace Column. In the background, the building forming the gateway to Hallesches Tor, 1881*

*Previous page: The Gendarmenmarkt with the playhouse and the French Cathedral, in the right foreground the "Königliche Seehandlung" (Royal Maritime Foundation), 1870*

In the last few decades of the last century these were replaced by new four and five-storey buildings. Now they no longer serve as residential buildings also accommodating wine bars and restaurants on their ground floors. Today, the old streets are lined by banks, offices, and insurance companies. The most striking change is that the old narrow-fronted lots have been replaced by spacious "quarters" six storeys high and topped by two additional storeys, set back from the façade. Schinkel's theatre building, which is now a concert hall, and the two churches resemble accessories which are virtually lost in the mountain-like perimeter development.

This pattern is repeated throughout the city, in the redesigned Friedrichstrasse and at Pariser Platz on the east side of the Brandenburg Gate and at Potsdamer Platz which, along with the Rond Point in Paris and London's Tower Bridge, was one of the most densely populated parts of the old Europe. Berlin has been restored, but the new Berlin only faintly resembles the old city which was destroyed in the bombs of World War II.

This is not necessarily to be understood as criticism of the new Berlin. The old Potsdamer Platz, the disappearance of which is still today mourned, was always a monstrosity, not a European square at all but an intersection of a large number of streets. It was dominated by three hotels and half a dozen places of amusement. The famous clock at its centre is actually the only thing which produces sentimental feelings. The Reichstag, in its third guise following Wallot's original and its modernisation by Baumgarten in the spirit of the Werkbund, is in its present design by Norman Foster perhaps for the first time a building which does not seem to require subservience. The Federal Chancellery designed by Axel Schultes promises to become an example of that symbolic architecture which, following Modernism, vulgar Modernism and Post-modernism, seeks a new language.

Once the building boom begun in the nineties ends, the greatest amount of building activity to be experienced in Berlin in the last one hundred years, an entirely new city will have emerged, in which only old names will be a reminder of what is past. The process of the emergence of this new Berlin is one followed with fascination and accompanied by goodwill and hope. Berlin is genuinely a city which never is, but is always in the process of becoming. This does not of necessity have to be a disadvantage. It is precisely this factor which sets Berlin apart from Rome, London and Paris. If these other European metropolises had been destroyed in World War II to the same extent as Berlin, the old Europe would have been the poorer for this – the incomparable beauty of these cities was part of its essence. Berlin never had this quality, for this it was too young, too late and too shapeless.

But it is this very factor which provides Berlin with the chance that its recreation will ultimately prove to be successful in the context of what is possible.

# CITY CASTLE

In the years leading up to the 15th century, Berlin was a lawless outpost at the edge of the Holy Roman Empire, mired in an endless cycle of plague, fire and theft. In 1411, Emperor Sigismund gave Frederick of the house of Hohenzollern title to the mark of Brandenburg and asked him to put an end to this ruinous state of affairs. After a series of spectacular battles with the Quitzow family of robber barons, Frederick quickly restored law and order to the unruly province. His successor Frederick II, also known as "Irontooth", extended Hohenzollern control by seizing private property, disbanding the courts and introducing his own tightly-controlled administration. To consolidate his authority in Berlin, he had a palace built on the west bank of the Spree in 1443, on the foundations of a crumbling city wall already over 200 years old.

Over the next four centuries, the descendants of Frederick II would add a jumble of annexes and additions to this medieval palace, with Emperor William II's picture gallery forming the final addition in 1904.

As palaces go, the original was not very impressive. Apart from the distinctive "pepper pot" towers that managed to survive into the 20th century, the rest was a forbidding, but unremarkable pile of Brandenburg brick. All this changed, however, with the ascension of Joachim II as Elector in 1535. Within five years, the ambitious ruler had transformed his residence into a richly decorated Renaissance palace, complete with a large central courtyard and Gothic chapel. He rejected traditional building materials in favour of imported sandstone and had master builder Konrad Krebs and Saxon architect Caspar Theyss oversee its construction. The Elector's pet project nearly emptied the family treasury.

A few more outbuildings were tacked on to the palace late in the 16th century, including the Apothecary's wing (1580-1595) and the Duchess House (1590), but, after these, no further improvements would take place for the next 100 years. A devastating fire in 1620, followed by repeated

*Above left: The White Salon (Weißer Saal), which was used for occasions of state, such as the opening of the German Reichstag. This magnificent ceremonial hall was originally designed by architect Stüler in 1844 and included reliefs by sculptor Otto Lessing*

*Above right: The Star Salon (Sternsaal), one of the palace salons remodelled by Karl Friedrich Schinkel in 1825*

*Below: A view of the palace's western gate during a visit by one of Graf Zeppelin's airships. To the right is the enormous monument to Emperor William I., photograph circa 1910*

military invasions marked the beginning of a period of devastation un-equalled in Berlin's short history. For three long decades, the mark of Brandenburg was plunged into a horrific abyss, as Austrian and Swedish armies took turns laying waste to the land. By the time Frederick William, the Great Elector, had at last brokered a peace with his enemies in 1644, the palace was an uninhabitable mess. Wooden planks had to be placed over parts of its walls to prevent its masonry from crumbling into the street. The rest of the half-deserted town was in no better shape.

The remarkable energy and talent the Great Elector was to lavish upon Berlin assured its recovery. He encouraged the immigration of skilled labourers from across Europe to help rebuild the town's shattered infra-structure and repopulate its surrounding farmland. Above all, he raised Berlin's profile as a trading centre by improving docking facilities on the River Spree and digging a canal that, via the city's waterways, would link the River Oder and River Elbe. The palace's grand Alabaster Salon, where the dancer Barberina would in later years dazzle Frederick the Great's court, was built at this time.

The Great Elector's legacy gave his son, Frederick III, the freedom to make several gigantic, Baroque additions to the family palace. Tired of his father's unrelenting austerity, the young prince was determined to live a life of luxury, surrounded with objects of beauty and culture. He put some of the century's best architects to work, hiring Jean de Bodt, Andreas Schlüter and Eosander von Göthe to design vast new wings that would extend the palace westwards, towards the opposite bank of the Spree Island. By the time von Göthe's triumphal western portal was completed in 1713, the castle had almost doubled its floorspace, sur-passing even the Bourbon palace in Versailles in size. No Hohenzollern who ruled thereafter would match the extravagance of Frederick III.

*The palace makes a brief comeback in the form of a four-storey canvas replica in the summer of 1993*

*Above: The ruined palace in May, 1945*

*Below: View across the Kupfergraben to the defunct Palace of the Republic. To the right are the former Royal Stables, designed by Ernst von Ihne, the same individual who remodelled many salons in the former city castle*

*Eosander von Göthe's majestic western gate with a portion of the National Monument in the foreground.*
*To the extreme left is the spire of the Berlin Cathedral*

Indeed, most of his heirs refused to remain within the palace's walls for any length of time. Frederick William I, who ruled between 1713 and 1740, preferred to stay in his rustic lodge in Königs Wusterhausen while his son, Frederick the Great, was far happier in his palace in Potsdam. As such, subsequent improvements to the palace were on-going, but relatively small in scale.

Karl Friedrich Schinkel had a hand in the redesign of a few interior salons in the 1820s, but the last, most impressive addition to the palace was Friedrich August Stüler's octagonal cupola, built in 1845, which rose 70 metres above the royal chapel at the western gate.

Shortly after William II ascended the throne in 1888, he decided to occupy the palace, which had lain vacant for years. While many of its cold, draughty rooms were refurbished to suit the young emperor's modern tastes, there was no room left for any more grandiose additions to the palace itself. Germany's last monarch had to satisfy his urge to build with the construction of a gaudy monument to his grandfather in front of von Göthe's western gate.

The National Monument was dedicated on March 22nd, 1897, and depicted Emperor William I on horseback in his general's uniform during

*Right: Otto Schönfelder and his wife enjoy a well-earned
retirement on the palace roof in the summer of 1930.
The pensioners, who were once employed by the emperor,
had been living in their little rooftop bungalow, since 1900*

*Below: The Eosander Portal during the palace's demolition on
October 14th, 1950. To the right is the gap where Schönfelder's
rooftop bungalow once stood. The western gate was dynamited
seventy-seven days later*

the Franco-Prussian war. Scattered around his feet was a collection of lions, field weapons, banners and winged Victories. A massive stone colonnade supporting yet more groups of bronzed figures in heroic poses surrounded the king on three sides. The cost of this sizeable work by Reinhold Begas was four million gold marks, a figure that provoked wide-spread grumblings of discontent among the emperor's subjects at the time. It would eventually take the East German government one full year to dismantle the site.

Eight years after the emperor's abdication in 1918, the palace became the property of the Prussian state. Parts of the palace served at various times as a science institute, museum, and soup kitchen, but much of the palace's 1,500 rooms remained vacant. Poorly maintained and largely ignored by the Nazi regime, the structure had by the 1930s deteriorated to the point where passers-by had to occasionally dodge crumbling bits of Baroque masonry that fell from its upper floors.

Apart from the odd stray bomb, the Imperial Palace remained relatively untouched throughout most of the war. But on the 3rd of February, 1945, a high-explosive shell landed on the north side of the building and deto-nated with disastrous effect. A fire quickly erupted, spreading throughout the entire first floor of the complex. Despite the intense heat of the flames, most of the Palace's metre-thick walls and much of Schlüter's magnificent sandstone façades remained structurally intact.

In October of 1949, the newly-created East German government per-mitted a Soviet film crew to shoot the epic "The End of Berlin" in and around the palace ruins. To add realism to their battle scenes, the film-makers brought several functioning artillery pieces with them and began firing live shells at the palace walls. They destroyed the stone cherubs that guarded the western gate and shattered over 200 window panes.

This cinematic act of vandalism was quickly followed by sinister rumours about the fate of the palace. Preservationists, knowing that the East German leadership wanted to be rid of the ruin, searched in vain for a letter Lenin was supposed to have written praising the palace's architectural merits. Meanwhile, the government pointed to the 50 million mark estimate for the reconstruction effort and said the money could be better spent elsewhere. For months, conflicting statements emerged from the State Planning Commission over the fate of the palace.

Finally on July 2nd, 1950, deputy prime minister Walter Ulbricht put an end to the speculation. He, who had lost several brothers in the Great War, felt little nostalgia for the emperor's last home. "The area around the ruins of the palace", he proclaimed, "will be made into a parade

The Berlin Cathedral and its simplified spires stand next to
the graffiti-daubed Palace of the Republic

ground where the will of the people for struggle and reconstruction can manifest itself." His preference was to erect a massive Stalinist tower like the ones he had seen in Moscow during his years of exile, but at the time his government lacked the financial means to embark on such an undertaking.

Because Ulbricht's decision to eradicate the palace was proving to be so controversial, the East German government wanted the demolition to be carried out as quickly as possible. Construction elsewhere in the eastern sector of Berlin was temporarily brought to a standstill as men and resources were diverted to the work of removing the shell-riddled palace. Demolition began in September 1950 with crews working in three shifts. The 365-year old Apothecary's Wing was the first to go up in smoke on September 6th. Next in line were Böhme's 17th century galleries at the south-west corner. Finally, at 3 p.m. on December 30th, the palace received its coup de grâce when 10,000 kilos of dynamite was detonated under Eosander von Göthe's 18th century arch.

The windswept site of the palace would remain empty for an entire generation. The National Reconstruction Plan that was launched in 1951 was chiefly concerned with rectifying the acute housing shortages brought about by the war and rebuilding what little industrial capacity that remained within the GDR's borders. Any plans to replace the palace with a more politically correct structure would have to wait until the communist state was more firmly established. Plans were put on hold once again in the early 1960s until the Berlin Wall and other projects of mass containment could be completed.

Only in 1973 was the time right for an ambitious construction project that would boost the public's ever-fading enthusiasm for the communist regime. SED party chairman Erich Honecker declared that a Volkskammer, or "people's parliament", would rise from the foundations of the palace. He decreed the construction of the parliamentary building, henceforth known as the "Palast der Republik" (Palace of the Republic).

From the outset, this new building was intended to be accessible to every citizen of the GDR. The architectural collective, under the leadership of Heinz Graffunder, sought to give the building a "bright, festive elegance" that would invite the common man inside.

In addition to its assembly chambers, the Palace of the Republic also included numerous restaurants, bars and cafés that offered inexpensive food not always available elsewhere in this shortage-plagued city. Its reception areas became a popular spot for East Germans who wished to celebrate graduations, marriages, retirements and other important

*Opposite: An early photo of the palace's Apothecary's Wing by Graf zu Lynar (shown in the background), which dated back to 1585*

*Above right: The Apothecary's Wing as it appeared around the turn of the century. The Kaiser Wilhelm Bridge had recently been built, seen in the foreground*

*Right: Zu Lynar's ruins fall to Ulbricht's dynamite in September of 1950*

dates. There was even an alley in the basement for bowling enthusiasts. Thus, for the next fourteen years East Berliners drank and bowled at the Palace of the Republic while their parliamentarians acted out the pretence of democratic socialism elsewhere in the building.

The winds of history swept across the site of the emperor's last home once again in 1990 when the East German state imploded. At first, the fate of the Palace of the Republic seemed destined to follow that of the state it once served. In September of 1990, the building was sealed off when health officials discovered it was filled with cancer-causing asbestos. Further inspections prompted city officials to declare the palace beyond salvation and decided it must go, even though other buildings in West Berlin, such as the International Congress Centre, had similar asbestos problems and were still in use.

Official plans to demolish the palace unleashed a wave of protest among former East Berliners, many of whom had fond memories of the place. They saw the decision as just one more attempt by the West Germans, "Wessis", to erase all evidence of the GDR's positive achievements.

But what would replace Honecker's Palace of the Republic? The Society to Promote the Imperial Palace, led by Hamburg businessman Wilhelm von Boddien, quickly raised several million dollars and pressed for the reconstruction of the Imperial Palace. It used some of that money in 1993 to erect a four-storey canvas replica of the palace to stimulate public awareness of its cause.

In the face of all this controversy, the Palace of the Republic was given a sudden reprieve. In 1995, orders for the destruction of the building were rescinded, at least temporarily, until the asbestos could be removed and a more permanent development plan for the square could be agreed upon.

*Opposite: Pre- and post-war views of the Apothecary's Wing, looking south-east*

*Below: From the opposite side of the Karl Liebknecht Bridge (former Kaiser Wilhelm Bridge) can be seen the Palace of the Republic. In the background to the right, covered in scaffolding, is the Friedrichswerder Church*

# FOREIGN OFFICE

The magnificent Baroque and Neo-Classical buildings that once lined the Wilhelmstrasse were part of an 18th century building campaign initiated by Prussia's "Soldier King", Frederick William I.

Midway through his reign, the king began distributing land south of the present-day Pariser Platz to members of Prussia's aristocracy. He sought to enhance the importance of his garrison town by inducing local nobility to leave their country estates and accept positions in the civil service and the army. These newcomers made the best of their new situation by securing the talent of noted architects such as Jean de Bodt, Friedrich Wilhelm Diterichs and Philipp Gerlach to design their city homes.

The residential palace on 76 Wilhelmstrasse was built during this period of expansion for Colonel Wolff Adolph von Pannewitz. His mansion, like that of his neighbour, War Councillor Johann Karl Stoltze, had a long, tranquil garden in the back that extended as far as Berlin's new customs wall. The palace was remodelled in 1805, and in 1819 was acquired by the Prussian State to house foreign minister Graf Bernstorff and his staff. For the next 126 years, the Pannewitz Palace would be better known as the Prussian and later German Foreign Office.

The palace's upper chambers temporarily lodged Otto von Bismarck in the years prior to and immediately after his becoming Chancellor in 1871. In all the years he lived there (1862-1876), Bismarck's household above the Foreign Office never shed its air of impermanence. Many rooms went without carpets; piles of books and other belongings lay in haphazard stacks on chairs and tables. Food usually arrived in caterer's wagons, rather than being prepared in the kitchen and on occasions when Bismarck had to entertain guests he chose to receive them in a nearby hotel.

Meanwhile, German foreign policy was conducted elsewhere in von Pannewitz's palace by a number of colourful individuals, among them

*Above left: A group of limousines clog the Wilhelmstrasse during the Foreign Office's annual New Year's Eve reception for Berlin's diplomatic community, January 12th, 1939*

*Above right: Joachim von Ribbentrop, head of Germany's Foreign Office during the Nazi years. This photo shows Ribbentrop in his newly-renovated headquarters, March 3rd, 1940*

*Above right: The German Foreign Office at 76 Wilhelmstrasse in 1898 during the administration of the mysterious Baron von Holstein*

*Below right: 76 Wilhelmstrasse showing severe damage, July 24th, 1945*

Baron Marschall von Bieberstein, who tried valiantly to deflect the emperor's muddled attempts at diplomacy. Perhaps the most mysterious figure of this era was senior counsellor Baron von Holstein. Despite repeated invitations, von Holstein travelled to the palace to meet the emperor just twice in the seventeen years he acted as his advisor. His reclusive habits and wily cunning earned him the nickname "monster of the labyrinth". When he was eventually fired in 1906, Baron von Holstein retaliated by leaking news of sexual escapades of the emperor's inner circle, a move that led to a series of scandalous trials that titillated Berliners for months on end.

By 1919, the Foreign Office had spread from 76 Wilhelmstrasse to absorb two neighbouring former palaces on the north side of the street. In the turbulent years that followed, Gustav Stresemann laboured from these expanded quarters to lead his government out of the diplomatic wilderness, a process he began by arranging a treaty with Bolshevik Russia.

The last high official to preside over Germany's foreign affairs on the Wilhelmstrasse was Joachim von Ribbentrop. A vain, intolerant man of less-than-sparkling intelligence, he carried out Hitler's foreign policy initiatives rather than attempt any of his own. Throughout the war, Ribbentrop's ministry became an increasingly useless appendage of the Nazi state, unable to deal on a diplomatic level with most of the world's nations. In the last days of the war, as Soviet rockets rained down with unremitting ferocity, foreign office officials were finally put to more useful work in the Wilhelmplatz, shovelling debris of fallen buildings into little iron wagons.

The shattered walls of the old palace lingered for a few years, but eventually it, and virtually everything else on the west side of the Wilhelmstrasse between the Voss Strasse and Pariser Platz were demolished by East German wrecking crews. After 1961, the spacious Foreign Office gardens became a free-fire zone behind the Berlin Wall. Its grounds were sown with land mines and soaked with herbicide so that nothing could grow and interfere with the border surveillance.

In the mid-1980s, construction workers descended on the vacant lot to erect a public housing project that was to be a showpiece of East German social policy. But before the project could be completed, the SED government collapsed. The project was allowed to continue nonetheless and today, von Pannewitz's estate has become an island of low-cost housing in what is now a very upscale neighbourhood.

An apparent complex, built using the prefabricate panels
so popular among East German engineers,
now occupies the Foreign Office site

# UNITED STATES EMBASSY

*Below: The imposing United States Embassy just south of the Brandenburg Gate in 1936. Built on the site of the old Blücher Palace, the building was rented out to aristocratic and other well-heeled tenants until the Americans bought it in 1930*

One of the most prestigious addresses in Berlin belonged for a few brief years to the septuagenarian General Gebhard von Blücher. His Neo-Baroque palace on 2 Unter den Linden was built with the assistance of Frederick William III, who wanted to thank the old general for his role in the defeat of Napoleon outside Leipzig in 1813. Blücher's palace was nothing if not spacious; it occupied the south-west corner of the Pariser Platz between the Brandenburg Gate and the Wrangel Palace on one side, as well as considerable frontage on the Königgrätzer Strasse (today Ebert-strasse) on the other.

The palace stood on this site for fifty years after von Blücher's death in 1819, and was then torn down to make way for a sophisticated rental property. The building, designed by Carl Richter, attracted a moneyed clientele who were willing to pay astronomical sums for a choice suite of rooms on Unter den Linden.

In 1930, Richter's building was sold to the United States government, which wanted a prestigious address of its own. Shortly after the sale was concluded, a devastating fire broke out and destroyed much of the building's interior. Eight years of costly renovations ensued. Only in 1939, just months before the onset of World War II, could the American diplomats move into their new embassy.

Hitler's declaration of war on Poland caught the Americans without an ambassador to Germany. The US State Department was still trying to find a suitable replacement for Ambassador William Edward Dodd, a Southern-er who had spent several fruitless years in Berlin trying to balance his distaste for the Nazi regime with the necessity of maintaining effective diplomatic and economic ties. In 1939, his duties were temporarily being carried out by his chargé d'affaires, Alexander Kirk. A well-liked member of Berlin's diplomatic community, Kirk kept in close contact with the infor-mal network of German dissidents who opposed Hitler's global designs.

The American Embassy continued to represent British and French interests after their own embassies had closed down for the duration of the war.

After the fall of 1939, relations between the Americans and the Nazi government deteriorated sharply. This atmosphere of distrust became apparent one day after a band of Gestapo men appeared at the embassy door. They had inspected the blueprints of the embassy's recent renovations and noticed a room labelled "Pulverkammer" (powder room). Convinced that this was a storage area for gunpowder, they demanded to be allowed inside to investigate. The Americans politely showed them the room, which turned out to be the ladies' toilet.

There was little to do at the embassy in the period between the outbreak of hostilities and the Americans' own declaration of war against the Axis powers. Most diplomatic functions had been cancelled, and, apart for a few news reporters working for the big radio networks and newspaper chains, there were few Americans left in Berlin to assist.

Later, after the British Royal Air Force had dropped their first bombs onto Berlin, the Americans tried to fend them off by painting a huge "USA" in white letters on their embassy roof. This measure proved futile: by war's end, the structure had been badly damaged.

After the war, the crumbling walls of the American Embassy, as well as those of the French Embassy, Deutsche Länderbank, and the Italianate homes north of the Pariser Platz were demolished by the Soviets, leaving just the Brandenburg Gate in bleak isolation. The embassy site became even more inaccessible after 1961, when it became part of "no-man's land" on the east side of the Berlin Wall.

After unification of the two Germanys, the Pariser Platz was once again a central point in a reunited Berlin. In 1993, the US government placed a plaque on the site of its former embassy, which read "The former and future site of the American Embassy in Berlin." The Californian architectural firm of Moore, Ruble & Yudell was awarded the commission for the new embassy's design and the US Congress subsequently approved 140 million DM for the embassy's construction.

The American Embassy's return to Unter den Linden and Pariser Platz has been complicated by a thorny security issue. In light of past attacks on its buildings overseas, the US government now requires a 30-metre "blast zone" to separate its embassies from adjoining buildings and streets. This requirement has set off a lively debate over how this buffer zone could be created in the midst of one of the most congested parts of the city.

*Above:*
*The abandoned American Embassy during the early days of Allied occupation*

*Below: Architect's rendering of the new embassy building, developed by Moore Ruble & Yudell of California*

*A post-war view of the embassy building,*
*shortly before it was razed to the ground*

*The vacant embassy site in winter 2000,*
*still unoccupied after almost 50 years.*
*To the left, behind the Brandenburg Gate,*
*is "Haus Sommer" designed by*
*Josef Paul Kleihues*

# ORDENS PALACE

One of the most striking residences to be built in the Friedrichstadt during the last years of the reign of Frederick William I was the Ordens Palace. Built on the north side of the Wilhelmplatz for the Grand Master of the Knights of St John in 1737, it was remodelled inside and out 90 years later for King Frederick William III's newly-married son, Prince Karl. The restoration was supervised by one of the most acclaimed architects of the time, Karl Friedrich Schinkel.

As part of his assignment to give the old mansion a more modern appearance, Schinkel had its sloped roof and dormer windows removed and its exterior walls reshaped in a simplified, Neo-Classical façade. Inside, he installed the first wrought-iron staircase in Berlin, using ideas he had gathered from a recent trip to England. A man of considerable talent, Schinkel even designed much of the furniture to grace Prince Karl's new salons. Some of his creations survive in museums to this day, including several giltwood armchairs that evoke the simple yet elegant furnishings of a Roman villa.

Once Prince Karl and his young bride had taken up residence, they proceeded to fill the ground floor with one of the greatest collections of armour and weaponry to be found in all of Germany. For many generations thereafter, the palace continued as a residence of Prussian nobility. Its last blue-blooded inhabitant was Prince Frederick Leopold of Prussia.

As part of a general trend that saw Prussia's aristocracy move out of their city palaces to make room for bureaucrats of the new Weimar Republic, in October of 1919 the Ordens Palace became headquarters to the recently founded Central Press Agency of the Reich Government. Operating under the auspices of the Foreign Office, the government's new information department became the forum whereby its policy and other official statements could be communicated to the world at large. Each day at twelve noon, a press conference would be held at the Garden

*Opposite: The Ordens Palace interior after its renovation by Karl Friedrich Schinkel*

*Below: Prince Karl's modernised residence on the north side of the Wilhelmplatz in 1890. The original palace was built in 1737 for the Grand Master of the Knights of St John*

Salon of the Ordens Palace. There, a government spokesman would read out the day's official pronouncements and field questions from members of the local, national and international press corps.

The Ordens Palace achieved true notoriety after 1933 when it merged with the former Prussian Ministry of Culture next door to become the Reich Ministry for Popular Enlightenment and Propaganda. The "Promi", as it came to be called, was headed by Dr. Joseph Goebbels, the master manipulator of fact and fiction. Upon his arrival, the propaganda chief immediately gutted the palace's ageing wood and plaster interior, saying "I must have around me clarity, cleanliness, and pure distinct lines. Twilight is repugnant to me." The result, according to a disapproving Albert Speer, was an interior completely redone in "ocean liner style".

Despite repeated and heavy aerial bombardment in the area, the Propaganda Ministry almost survived the war. In fact, by 1945, it was virtually the only building on the Wilhelmplatz with its four walls intact. But in broad daylight on March 13th, a lone parachute mine released from an RAF bomber drifted over the Wilhelmplatz, landed on the palace's roof, and blew the entire structure to pieces.

For many years, the site of the Ordens Palace was used as a parking lot. In 1989, the East German government began construction of an apartment complex, but work was interrupted with the demise of the communist government later that year. The project has since been completed and the building is now occupied by residential tenants in the upper floors, with a youth recreation centre at street level.

*Above: Goebbels' propaganda is replaced by that of the Russians. The ruined Propaganda Ministry next to a Soviet message to the people (far left) in 1945: "The strength of the Red Army lies in the fact that it neither feels nor can feel racial hatred of other peoples, including the German people, that it has been trained in the spirit of equality of all peoples and races, in the spirit of respect for the rights of other peoples."*

*Opposite: Even by contemporary standards, the successor to Prince Karl's residence is stunning in its mediocrity*

*Right: A narrow-gauge railway carts off the bombed remains of the Propaganda Ministry in 1948*

*Far right: From palace to parking lot. A scrap of greenery is all that is left of Prince Karl's home by 1986*

# REICHSTAG

The first German parliament, or Reichstag, owed its existence to the founder of modern Germany, Otto von Bismarck. Unfortunately for the new parliamentarians, however, their role was just so much window-dressing — Bismarck had written important parts of the constitution so that he as Chancellor could ignore any vote in the Reichstag that went against him. The one area the parliamentarians did have control over was finance, but they often let themselves be manipulated into approving unpopular expenditure. Indeed, Reichstag as an institution was considered to be of such limited importance that, for the first 12 years of its existence, elected members did not even have a place of their own to meet.

Eventually a site was found and on June 9th, 1884, Emperor William I grudgingly laid the foundation stone of the new Reichstag building in the north-east corner of the Tiergarten. It would take 10 years and 28 million marks to complete. The result was splendid sandstone structure executed in a Neo-Renaissance style. Mounted above its Italianate walls was a great glass dome, through which the sun's rays could pass to illuminate the chambers within.

Despite the countless sessions of witty and often penetrating debate, the Reichstag remained subordinate to the ultimate authority of the Chancellor and the periodic whims of the Emperor. Never, at any time in the years leading up to 1914, did this quarrelsome potpourri of political parties ever manage to come together and present a unified challenge to the Crown.

In 1918, when the Emperor abdicated, the Reichstag at last became a genuine source of democratic power in Germany. Between 1919 and 1933 a number of outstanding men and women legislated and debated in its chambers, in a flawed parliamentary system that allowed even the tiniest and most extreme political party a say in the running of the country. It was not an easy time, but through all this the Reichstag gained in

*Opposite: Reichstag reading room, circa 1920*

*Below: An early view of the Reichstag building, designed by Paul Wallot and completed in 1894*

importance and was able to pursue a successful foreign and domestic policy from 1923 to 1929. These were known as "the good years", and they were not to last.

By 1930, a new threat to the young Weimar Republic had emerged — Adolf Hitler's National Socialist Workers' Party. Pandering to Germany's sense of economic insecurity, xenophobia and nostalgia for social order, Hitler bullied his way onto the political stage. He used the democratic mechanism of the Reichstag to bring his party to power, but once there, he refused to leave.

On February 27th, 1933, a panic-stricken citizen burst into the Brandenburg Gate guardroom. He had been sent by a policeman to alert the guards that someone had broken into the Reichstag. He breathlessly reported that he had seen a man running from window to window with a flaming torch in his hand. The policeman had fired off a few rounds from his revolver but every shot missed; the arsonist was still running amok.

After hearing his story, one of the Brandenburg Gate guards picked up a phone and dialled the fire brigade. The fire trucks raced to the scene, but by then it was too late; flames were raging throughout the building.

In the years following the blaze, the Reichstag lay idle, its use as a democratic forum made obsolete by the increasingly totalitarian rule of the Nazi party.

*Above: The Reichstag's bullet-scarred front entrance in July 1945, showing graffiti left by Russian soldiers*

*Right: The Reichstag shortly after its capture by the Red Army. Its ruins soon became the scene of a flourishing black market*

On April 29th, 1945, the old parliament building fell victim to yet more depredations during a final, desperate battle between the advancing Russians and the remnants of the SS Nordland Battalion. The German defenders were holed up in the Reichstag basement while the Red Army opposed them from the ruins of the Kroll Opera House. After a day of bitter resistance, the Nordland troops were silenced when the Russians ringed the building with 90 heavy guns and opened fire. Within hours the Soviet Union's Red Banner could be seen fluttering atop the Reichstag entrance.

It may have taken ten years to build the Reichstag, but it would take another fourteen years to restore it. Reconstruction work began in 1957 and did not stop until 1971, exactly 100 years after the first Reichstag convened. The chief architect, Paul Baumgarten, followed a path of "purified modernism" when designing the Reichstag's interior. His approach obliterated all but a few of the building's surviving Wilhelmine chambers.

Over the next two decades, the updated Reichstag served in a distinctly anti-climactic role as an occasional meeting place for committees of the Bundestag and Bundesrat as well as other parliamentary groups of the West German government.

In 1991, just a year after unification, the Bundestag voted by the narrowest of margins to move the nation's capital from Bonn back to Berlin. As a consequence, full parliamentary sessions resumed at the Reichstag in September 1999, after a 66-year hiatus. The Reichstag's interior has once again been reshaped — this time in favour of a return to Wallot's original floorplan, with one strikingly modern innovation.

A new glass dome, designed by architect Sir Norman Foster, was commissioned to replace the Reichstag's long-lost cupola. This 47 metre-high dome, completed in the fall of 1998, features a spiral pedestrian ramp that corkscrews its way up to the summit. Suspended from the dome's apex is a funnel of angled mirrors that descends like a great glittering icicle to illuminate the plenary chamber below. The new cupola is intended as the physical embodiment of Germany's political ideal: an open and transparent government of the people.

*In 1995, Christo, a Bulgarian-born American artist, wrapped the Reichstag in 10,000 square metres of aluminised plastic film. The stunt cost 15 million marks and attracted five million visitors*

*Opposite above: The underused German Reichstag at the edge of a divided city in 1986*

*Below: The debris of war has, half a century later, been replaced with the debris of rebirth. The reconditioned Reichstag receives the finishing touches to its grounds in winter, 2000*

# ERNST REUTER PLATZ

The sandy lane that originally wended its way through this part of the city in the 18th century connected the royal hunting grounds of the Tiergarten with Queen Sophie Charlotte's Palace to the west. However, during Berlin's rapid expansion phase in the 1880s and 90s, this quiet road was transformed into a bustling gateway to the city's rapidly-expanding western suburbs. Called the "Knie" (Knee) for the six street corners that protruded into the square like bent limbs, its centre island included an entrance to a subway station designed by famed architect Alfred Grenander.

After World War I, the city government formed a special corps of traffic police to handle the swarms of Horches, Delages, Mercedes and Opels that started to sweep through busy city intersections like the Knie. In summer, a white-coated officer could be seen in the middle of the square, waving his arms at the mad rush of automobiles. When winter approached, he would change into a vivid, blue-coated tunic. During the Christmas season, motorists — and perhaps a few grateful pedestrians who owed their lives to the officer's quick intervention — would place wrapped presents of cognac and cigars at his feet.

The volume of traffic around the Knie continued to rise as Germany overcame its political and economic setbacks, only to decline once again after the outbreak of war. Beginning in 1939, growing numbers of cars were either taken off the road for lack of gasoline or commandeered by the military for service elsewhere in the Reich. The square itself suffered much damage on May 1st, 1945, as local defenders engaged in a last-minute artillery duel with members of the Soviet 219th Tank Brigade.

In 1953, the Knie's name was changed to Ernst Reuter Platz in honour of West Berlin's first mayor. In the years that followed, city planners wondered what to do with the newly renamed square and the acres of ruins that surrounded it. One recurring idea was to create a "City Band" of modern buildings that would stretch from the Ernst Reuter Platz in the

west to the Alexanderplatz in the east. The nearby Hansaviertel development that was launched on the site of the 1957 International Building Exhibition (Internationale Bauausstellung Berlin 1957) was meant to be a step in this direction.

That same year the Federal Government and West Berlin Senate jointly announced an international competition called "Capital City Berlin" which was intended to provide a master blueprint for a city-wide reconstruction effort. Architects and city planners from around the world were invited to submit a plan that reflected "visions of the unity and visual coherence of united Berlin as a capital city". The organisers chose to ignore the fact that half of Berlin was currently in communist hands and that the last attempt to jointly plan the city had ended in total failure nine years earlier.

The competition attracted a flood of grand designs, some of frightening proportions. Le Corbusier's submission called for a canyon of American-style skyscrapers, including a 65-storey "House of Bureaucracy", that would have put most of central Berlin in deep shade.

A fragment of the post-modernist paradise that never came to pass can be seen today in the tall skyscrapers that surround the Ernst Reuter Platz. The severity of the towers was offset by 62 fountains designed by Werner Düttmann and installed in 1960. The fountains were shut down in 1993 in a cost-saving measure, but the dry spell ended six years later after Ernst Reuter's son Edzard set forces in motion to get the water flowing again.

The windswept expanse of the Ernst Reuter Platz is transformed once a year into a wild gathering of young people in outlandish costumes and various stages of undress. Masquerading as a political demonstration, the annual "Love Parade" can more accurately be described as Berlin's answer to Mardi-Gras. What began as a public nuisance in 1989 has grown to become an important source of revenue to Berlin, as well as a lot of fun for over a million revellers. Around every July 11th at roughly 2 p.m., a lively procession of floats begins at the Ernst Reuter Platz to the deafening blast of techno music and heads eastward to the Victory Column, where it meets another procession coming from the Brandenburg Gate.

*Previous page: One of the more distinctive pre-war buildings that bordered the Knie (now the Ernst Reuter Platz). This structure originally housed offices of the Deutsche Petroleum AG*

*Above right: The landmark building after the collapse of the "Third Reich". In the foreground is one of the lampposts designed by Albert Speer. They were the only creation of his to survive the war*

*Below right: One of the modernist office towers that now ring the square*

# BRANDENBURG GATE

In 1738, Frederick William I had a wall built around Berlin in an effort to frustrate both the customs cheaters who were denying him his money and the soldiers who attempted to desert his garrison. The wall was pierced at 14 points with simple town gates which collected duty on the people and goods entering the city. The baroque tollhouse that provided access to the newly laid out Unter den Linden and the royal palace beyond was known as the Brandenburg Gate.

The famous monument that has since become Berlin's trademark was erected a half century later on the orders of King Frederick William II. Modelled by Carl Gotthard Langhans after the Propylaeum on the Acropolis in Athens, the new Gate brought a touch of Neo-Classical grandeur to the city's western approaches. At the time of its completion in 1791, the Gate's yellowish-grey stonework was a dazzling white. Whether this white exterior was paint, glaze, or some other substance is something we may never know, since this outer coating was completely scrubbed off in 1956 during a misguided GDR-era restoration project.

The monument's twelve Doric columns were topped in 1794 by Johann Gottfried Schadow's flowing-robed goddess and her horse-drawn chariot. The Quadriga remained in place for only 13 years before it was taken down again by Napoleon's troops and sent to Paris as war booty. When it was recovered in 1814 after Prussia's successful war of liberation, Karl Friedrich Schinkel introduced a new staff for the goddess, which included the Prussian eagle and his newly designed Iron Cross.

After the old customs wall was demolished in the 1860s, Langhans' monument served a purely ornamental role, becoming a focal point for countless military parades, royal processions and other public ceremonies.

*View of the Gate in 1940.*
*The foreground shows a portion of the*
*French embassy's Neo-Classic portico*

*Opposite above: Pre-war view of the Brandenburg Gate looking westward to the Tiergarten. The monument was designed by Silesian master builder Carl Gotthard Langhans on orders of King Frederick William II and completed in 1791*

*Below: View of the Langhans' Gate looking south from the Königgrätzer Strasse (today Ebertstrasse)*

*Right: July 7th, 1945. The mangled Quadriga atop the Gate shortly before it was pulled down by the Russians and replaced with a simple red flag*

The war years subjected the Gate not only to damage by bombs, but also to a steady pilfering of its component parts. On February 11th, 1943, the monument had its copper roofing removed for military use, but the Quadriga itself was spared. Two years later, only fragments of the goddess and her mangled bronze chariot remained. They were soon swept away by the Soviets and replaced with a single red flag.

In the late 1950s, the two halves of the divided city struck a deal whereby East Berlin would restore the Gate's battle-scarred masonry while West Berlin would restore the Quadriga. A copy of Schadow's sculpture was duly crafted from a set of moulds of the goddess, chariot and horse team made during the war, then left in the Soviet zone for the East Germans to retrieve. The Quadriga then returned to its historic place atop the Gate — but only after the communists sawed off the goddess's Iron Cross and Prussian eagle in her wreath.

Three years later on a sunny August day in 1961, over five thousand Berliners gathered at the Brandenburg Gate to watch East German construction crews sink a line of concrete posts across the western side of the monument. Everyone knew what was about to happen — rumours had been circulating throughout the city all summer. The construction crews, working under the supervision of East German military and police units, then began to unroll coils of barbed wire from their drums and draped them across the line of newly planted posts, creating what would soon be known the world over as the Berlin Wall.

During John F. Kennedy's historic visit to Berlin in June, 1963, the West Berlin Senate built a raised dais next to the Brandenburg Gate so

*Left: View of the burning city centre in May, 1945, with the Gate to the right*

the US President could look out over the newly-erected Wall. The East Germans promptly obstructed his view by erecting huge red cloth banners between the Gate's columns.

For the next 26 years, other, less famous visitors to Berlin would make their own pilgrimage to the sealed-off Gate. On the Tiergarten side, double-decker tour buses would sit with their motor running while American and British passengers took a moment to gawk eastward. Just a few hundred metres away, visiting Vietnamese and North Korean dignitaries would snap off shots from their side of the barricade on the Pariser Platz.

On November 9th, 1989, after a series of failed attempts to stem the tide of mass emigration through their newly liberalised East Bloc neighbours, the GDR government lifted the last of its travel restrictions. It was an act that signalled the end of the Wall and ultimately of the communist regime itself. Six weeks later, Chancellor Helmut Kohl walked in the rain through the newly-opened Brandenburg Gate to greet his East German counterpart, Hans Modrow. Their historic words of conciliation were soon replaced by the sound of thousands of "wall woodpeckers", whose innumerable chisels in no time stripped the once-formidable barrier around the Gate of its last graffito.

*Above left: The new Quadriga, prior to its installation atop the Gate in the fall of 1958*

*Above right: The goddess Victoria anticipates the arrival of her second horse. Her staff has been freshly shorn of its iron cross and eagle*

*The new buildings that flank the Brandenburg Gate match the height and form of their pre-war ancestors*

*Below: A contemporary view of Langhans' monument looking south to the construction cranes around Leipziger Platz*

# NEW GUARDHOUSE

Freed at last from the distractions of the Napoleonic Wars, King Frederick William III felt in 1814 that the time had finally come to rebuild his royal residence. One of his first decisions was to order a new headquarters for his palace guard. This would be the first building of consequence to rise in the city since Napoleon's troops first marched into Berlin in 1806. The prestigious project was awarded to the up-and-coming architect from Neuruppin, Karl Friedrich Schinkel. It was the 34-year-old designer's first major commission and, in the opinion of many, his finest achievement.

Before construction could begin however, the old Kanonierwache that had for years housed troops attached to the Zeughaus (armoury) had to be pulled down and a fetid moat known as the Grüne Graben covered over. In its place, Schinkel introduced an almost perfectly square building erected in a design inspired by Roman military architecture. The architect included two rows of six Doric columns at its entrance which, after 1822, were flanked by Christian Rauch's statues of two Prussian heroes, generals Scharnhorst and Bülow.

The architect had originally intended for the New Guardhouse to be integrated into a broader concept that would involve the re-landscaping of the neighbouring royal garden, but the King rejected his plans. His final, more modest layout set the royal guardhouse in among a grove of chestnut trees and pedestrian walkways, interspersed with statuary and captured enemy cannons.

However, Schinkel's carefully designed grounds were to serve a purpose that neither the young architect nor the king envisioned. The copse of chestnut trees behind the New Guardhouse became known by local police as an "assembly point" for illicit encounters. Among the prostitutes that loitered among the trees were a few of the king's own soldiers who

*Opposite: Heinrich Tessenow's remodelled interior in 1931.*
*An open skylight exposed the inner chamber to the*
*elements*

*Below: Karl Friedrich Schinkel's Neo-Classical masterpiece built*
*in 1816–18 to house Frederick William III's palace guard*

would sell themselves for a few groschen to supplement their meagre wages.

The guardhouse served as a military garrison and prisoner holding cell for exactly one hundred years. After the emperor's abdication, the New Guardhouse was transformed into a reception area for various civic events. Then, in 1931, it was redesigned by Heinrich Tessenow and designated as a war memorial for soldiers who lost their lives during World War I.

Tessenow adopted a Minimalist approach and created a memorial chamber that contained nothing but a black stone plinth topped with a silver wreath at its centre. A circular opening in the roof exposed the chamber to the elements.

Once a year, top-ranking members of the German armed forces would gather in Tessenow's remodelled vault to observe Hero's Remembrance Day. The last official observation took place on March 11th, 1945, when a desultory gathering of Nazi big shots and Wehrmacht holdouts made one last visit to the old guardhouse.

Adolf Hitler was not among them. He had emerged from the seclusion of his bunker to make a rare trip to the eastern front, which at the time was perilously close to the city limits.

Damaged by shellfire during the Red Army's final assault on the city, the guardhouse narrowly escaped demolition after the war. The director of the office for museums in the communist half of Berlin called for the monument's immediate destruction. "The existence of a memorial, patronised by the Nazis, immediately in front of the House of Culture of the Soviet Union is a disgrace." Prominent members of the FDJ, the communist youth organisation, agreed. "We consider it better for spatial reasons that the ruins of the memorial should disappear as soon as possible." Despite their urging, the monument was left to crumble for another 20 years.

The SED government had lost some of its antipathy towards Schinkel's monument and ordered its full restoration in 1950. From 1960 until the last days of the East German regime, the New Guardhouse served as a memorial for "Victims of Fascism and Militarism". Tessenow's damaged

*The New Guardhouse on July 8th, 1945.*
*A Russian signpost provides directions to the*
*Reichstag, Potsdam and Nauen*

black column and wreath was replaced with a crystal cube and an eternal flame. In an odd resumption of pre-war custom, military units returned to stand guard at the monument's entrance, with a goose-stepping detachment of the Friedrich Engels Honour Guard remaining at its post until the unit was dissolved in September, 1990.

After Unification, the New Guardhouse was redesigned once again. The decision to create a new memorial came from Chancellor Helmut Kohl himself. He wanted a memorial that would represent all victims of man's inhumanity to man, including not only victims of war, but those of terrorism, political tyranny and racial persecution.

Rejecting designs that evoked "hopelessness", Helmut Kohl finally settled on a sculpture based on noted Berlin artist Käthe Kollwitz. He chose an enlarged version of Kollwitz's "Mother", sculpted in 1937, preferring it for its evocation of "indestructible humanity".

The New Guardhouse is now patrolled by units of the Bundeswehr's Guards Battalion.

*Above left: The People's Army of the GDR struts past the Neue Wache in March, 1966. A few years later, the East Germans finally got around to renovating the monument's interior*

*Above right: The monument receives its post-Unification makeover. Tessenow's skylight makes a return appearance, illuminating an enlarged version of Käthe Kollwitz's 1937 sculpture "Mother"*

*A 1972 view of the New Guardhouse in its role as memorial to the "Victims of Fascism and Militarism"*

*Below: Karl Friedrich Schinkel's Neue Wache today: a symbol
of remembrance and hope*

# KEMPERPLATZ

Today, an onlooker inhaling the exhaust fumes of cars speeding around the corner of the Tiergartenstrasse and the B 96 access ramp could scarcely imagine the tranquillity of the Kemperplatz as it was in its earlier days.

The square was named after the first coffee-house to open here in 1725. The "Kemperhof" was the first of many establishments to serve coffee, chocolate and wine to Berlin's cityfolk, who passed by on their way to the green refuge of the Tiergarten.

Around 1850, the last vacant lots in this quiet part of the world were bought up by wealthy financiers, triggering a wave of villa-building that soon transformed the area into what came to be known as the "Millionaires' Quarter". The Oppenheim family and other banking dynasties such as the Rothschilds and Fürstenbergs shared their verdant neighbourhood with a distinguished assortment of academics, artists, and top-ranking politicians. At one point the Brothers Grimm lived around the corner on the Lennéstrasse; Karl Marx stayed just stone's throw away during his visit to Berlin in 1861.

Towards the end of the 19th century, a wide promenade leading north of the Kemperplatz was carved out of the Tiergarten on orders of Emperor William II. He requested the passage be lined with around 70 statues of Prussia's rulers and their serving ministers. Empress Augusta and others tried to dissuade him, considering the tribute to be a bit overdone, but he refused to listen. Shortly after the monuments were installed on the newly-christened Siegesallee, Berliners began referring to the passage as "plaster avenue".

A few years later, Kemperplatz itself was updated with flower gardens, a public fountain and a statue of the legendary Danish warrior Roland. The red granite figure, 3.75 metres high, was completed by the renowned sculptor Otto Lessing in 1902.

*Above left: The Siegesallee in 1901. A group of strollers admire a statue of Margrave Albrecht II*

*Above right: The Kemperplatz and its statue of Roland looking north up the shattered Siegesallee after the war*

Above: The Kemperplatz and its statue
of Roland in 1938, looking south from the
Tiergarten onto the Tiergartenstrasse

Below: The Kemperplatz seen from
the opposite direction in 1946, looking
north to the defoliated Tiergarten.
Directly ahead is the Siegesallee

After World War I, the neighbourhood's wealthy homeowners started to flee the growing waves of noise and traffic for the more restful environs of Wilmersdorf and other west-end communities. Many were bought out by foreign powers seeking a respectable place to house their diplomatic missions. Thus the "Millionaires' Quarter" had, by the 1930s, become the "Diplomatic Quarter". As the sobering hand of Nazidom pervaded the city, embassy parties around the Kemperplatz became one of the last places still offering the opportunity of uninhibited fun.

The square would have been eliminated entirely, had the war not interrupted things. The statue of Roland was to be removed and the emperor's Siegesallee substantially widened to make way for a north-south axis road. The square's reprieve was brief however. By 1945 Roland was in ruins and the rows of statuary on the Siegesallee fared no better. While Lessing's dismembered hero disappeared for good, a resourceful state curator, Hinnerk Schaper, saved what he could of the emperor's marbles.

Sensing that much of the broken statuary was headed for Teufelsberg, the mountain of rubble that was the final destination of many a Berlin ruin, the curator took it upon himself to bury a number of the shattered fragments nearby in the gardens of Bellevue Palace. His hope was that a day would come when the marbles could resurface, when Germany had become more accepting of its monuments to the past.

In 1979 the statues were dug up from their graves and stored at the Hallesches Ufer, in a picturesque building that once served as Berlin's first sewage pumping station. To this day, the old waterworks continues as a sanctuary, protecting the emperor's marbles from the ravages of acid rain and other airborne pollutants. These statues share the space with other original monuments, which have been removed from their locations across Berlin and replaced with more durable cement stand-ins.

Today, nothing remains of the original Kemperplatz except its name. Its gardens and fountain have long since been paved over to make a four-way intersection, while the Siegesallee was reduced to a narrow path that leads to the Soviet War Memorial. An extension to the Entlastungsstrasse was built just to the west of the old promenade in the 1960s after the Berlin Wall blocked off other north-south roads nearby.

Today, the square serves as an access point to the new B96 tunnel that burrows its way for 2.4 kilometres beneath the Tiergarten and River Spree. The Kemperplatz, as a result, has become busier than ever. The Tiergarten and those who use it have nonetheless benefited from this new arrangement. No longer is the park divided by the busy Entlastungsstrasse; rendered obsolete by the new tunnel, this Cold War highway is has been ripped up and absorbed into the greenery of Berlin's central park.

*Opposite: Marble effigies of Kaiser William I (left),*
*Margrave Johann II and Margrave Otto II contemplate their*
*new surroundings in 1946*

*Below: The Kemperplatz in 2000. The Entlastungsstrasse,*
*seen covered with construction material, will soon be reclaimed*
*by the Tiergarten*

# GENDARMENMARKT

The Gendarmenmarkt takes its name from Frederick William I's regiment of the Gens d'Armes, which was stationed here in 1736. The twin churches that dominate the north and south sides of the square were built somewhat earlier, in the first decade of the 18th century, in tribute to the French and German Reformations. The French and German Cathedrals' distinctive drum-like cupolas were added 80 years later by Karl von Gontard, who drew his inspiration from the church of St Mary in the Piazza del Popolo in Rome.

To the west of the square stands the Schauspielhaus, on the site of the original French Comedy House built in 1703 to entertain the Prussian aristocracy. The old comedy house was rebuilt in 1802 by Carl Gotthard Langhans but shortly afterwards a disastrous fire, probably caused by a workman's unattended lamp, reduced the structure to ruins. The flames were so intense that they spread across the street and consumed E.T.A. Hoffmann's home on 56 Charlottenstrasse. Damage was extensive and destroyed all the sets for Hoffmann's opera "Undine" as well as those created for Mozart's "The Magic Flute".

Karl Friedrich Schinkel, the same architect whose breathtaking canvas backdrops were lost in the fire, won the contract to build a grander, more fireproof structure. Entirely rebuilt along Greek classical lines, he designed a majestic façade of alternating pilaster-piers and tall windows that permitted a maximum presence of natural light. His finished product caused an international sensation and assured the architect a lifetime of lucrative commissions.

*View of the square in 1939 looking north to the French Cathedral. Schinkel's Schauspielhaus, which opened to the public in 1821, is seen to the left*

*Right: The Gendarmenmarkt after the war. The incinerated remains of the Sixth Panzer Division can still be seen in the foreground*

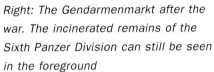

The Schauspielhaus was always a popular venue for instrumental music, but it also staged numerous plays by Goethe and Schiller, as well as countless operatic performances.

The long-dominant position of Italian opera was toppled here in 1821 when Carl Maria von Weber's "Der Freischütz" premièred. Weber's bridesmaid's song "Wir winden dir den Jungfernkranz" (We Weave you the Bridal Wreath) became a public sensation. That summer, Weber's lyrics could be heard on everyone's lips, from hackney-carriage drivers to scullery maids.

The Schauspielhaus continued into the 20th century as a state theatre that chiefly played classical dramas. In 1927, a young actor called Maria Magdalena von Losch made an early appearance in Max Reinhardt's production of "The Taming of the Shrew". The 26-year-old Berliner, better known as Marlene Dietrich, would in just a few years go on to become an icon of her age.

Throughout the war — despite the periodic ravages of aerial bombardment — the Schauspielhaus never stopped giving performances to Berliners. During one such attack, on December 16th, 1943, several incendiary devices struck the playhouse, setting its timbered roof and parquet floors ablaze. Nevertheless, the main hall was soon patched up and theatre productions resumed as before.

Risk to theatregoers intrepid enough to attend wartime performances peaked during the last days of the "Third Reich" as General Johann von Krukenberg's 6th Panzer Division faced the Red Army in street-by-street

*Left: The cupola of the French Cathedral in flames following an air raid in 1943*

combat in the city's downtown core. On Easter Sunday, with the Russians only a few blocks down the street and the surrender of Berlin just days away, the Berlin Philharmonic under the directorship of Robert Heger played "Aïda" in the partially ruined playhouse.

The end of the war found the Gendarmenmarkt within the Soviet zone of occupation. For the next 30 years, the twin churches and Schinkel's playhouse were fenced off and forgotten. From the crevices of their crumbling pediments, whole trees took root, some of which grew to an impressive size. Finally, in 1976, systematic work began on restoration, a project that continued intermittently for the next decade and a half.

While the old playhouse has continued to hold many excellent performances since its restoration, none was as dramatic as that held on the night of October 2nd, 1990, when the final act of the East German regime was played out. Lothar de Maizière, East Germany's first and last democratically-elected Prime Minister, stood on the stage before a packed house and said, "In a few moments, the German Democratic Republic accedes to the Federal Republic of Germany. It is an hour of great joy. It is the end of many illusions. It is a farewell without tears."

With that, Kurt Masur, hero of the popular unrest that toppled the communist regime, rose to conduct Beethoven's Ninth Symphony.

*Opposite: The German Cathedral in 1986, receiving its long-awaited restoration*

*Below: The Gendarmenmarkt today. The French Cathedral's spire dominates the skyline, as new construction continues to revitalise this long-dormant part of the city*

# TIERGARTEN

Opposite: Christian Friedrich Tieck's Lion Bridge (Löwenbrücke). The footbridge dates back to 1837, a time when landscape architect Peter Lenné first gave the Tiergarten its romantic English motif

Below: By the time this photo was taken in 1933, the king's hunting parties in the Tiergarten had been replaced by leisurely equestrian outings of Berlin's upper-middle class

Wildlife has abounded in the fertile land now occupied by Berlin ever since the last glaciers receded here over 10,000 years ago. For millennia, these forests and meadows provided a rich hunting ground for Brandenburg's early nomadic tribes. Much later, a portion of this area that lay south of the River Spree between the present-day Jägerstrasse and the village of Lietzow (now Charlottenburg) became the exclusive hunting ground for generations of Hohenzollern princes. It was known as the Tiergarten.

While the exact dimensions of this royal hunting preserve were only defined after 1465, fences were eventually put up and stiff fines meted out to those who dared to poach in the Prince's domains. During the reign of Johann Georg in the 1570s, anyone caught killing one of his rabbits was fined 50 talers. Shooting one of his bucks brought a 500 taler penalty — a staggering sum at the time. The transformation from hunting ground to public park began when Queen Sophie Charlotte had a palace

built for her to the west of the Tiergarten. In the years that followed, the wilds that separated her residence from Berlin were gradually tamed and turned into parkland for the aristocracy and other leisure classes to enjoy. In 1742, Hans Georg Wenzeslaus von Knobelsdorff made the first attempt to civilise the old hunting grounds by designing ponds, French-style labyrinths and star-shaped gardens.

He was so taken with the park's peaceful beauty that he built his own house here. The brother of Frederick II, Prince August Ferdinand, eventually demolished it and had it replaced with the Neo-Classic Schloss Bellevue in 1785.

Even before it was fully converted to public use, the Tiergarten became a green refuge for strollers seeking temporary escape from the narrow, often filthy streets of old Berlin. During the reign of Frederick the Great, the northern edge of the park became a popular place where one could obtain lemonade, weak beer and other refreshments from tents set up on park lawns. Later on, these garden restaurants were replaced with permanent coffee houses such as "Zum ewigen Zelte" (The Eternal Tents) or the "Hofjäger" to the south. This latter establishment was once a farmstead that belonged to the royal gamekeeper and occupied an idyllic location next to the Landwehr Graben at the end of what is now the Tiergartenstrasse.

The present-day layout of the Tiergarten can be attributed to the renowned landscape architect Peter Joseph Lenné. Working at times in collaboration with Karl Friedrich Schinkel, Lenné spent 15 years perfecting its design. Drainage of neighbouring marshland began in 1832 and landscaping continued for the next eight years. For his efforts, Lenné was paid 7,000 talers and was given a plot of land at the corner of the present-day Ebertstrasse and Lennéstrasse.

Not long after he had put the finishing touches on Berlin's central park, Lenné focused his attentions on a new project in its south west corner, in a field once inhabited by the king's pheasants. There, on August 1st, 1844, Germany's first zoo opened to the public. For the next 50 years, Berlin's Zoological Gardens would remain the largest in the world.

By the late 19th century, the Tiergarten had been completely hemmed in by Berlin's urban sprawl. Inside the park, busts of Second Reich notables and assorted other statuary began popping up like so many marble mushrooms along its newly-widened promenades. The largest monument by far was the Victory Column (Siegessäule), a massive stone pillar erected in 1873 to celebrate the military victories that led to the founding of the Second Reich. Berliners looking up at the column's seven-ton bronze Goddess of Victory would affectionately refer to her as "Berlin's heaviest female".

In preparation for Hitler's future Reich capital, Germania, city work crews moved the Goddess and her column at great expense from the

*The partially-destroyed Lion Bridge in 1946. By then, the Tiergarten's forests had almost completely disappeared*

Königsplatz to the centre of the park on the east-west axis road. The move saved the monument from almost certain destruction when twelve years later, in April of 1945, its former site in front of the Reichstag was to become the scene of particularly intense fighting.

Like the city that surrounded it, the Tiergarten was a shambles after the war. Burned out military vehicles and disabled artillery pieces lay scattered in every direction.

Lawns had been ploughed over to grow potatoes, evidence of how Berliners had turned to farming for survival. But the most obvious and for many the most distressing result of war was the park's sudden lack of greenery. Virtually all of its 200,000 trees had been shattered by artillery fire, felled for emergency airstrips, or chopped up by local residents in need of firewood to heat their homes.

The early post-war years were spent restoring gas, electrical and water supplies to the devastated city, but on March 17th, 1949, West Berlin mayor Ernst Reuter launched the Tiergarten's rebirth by planting the park's first post-war linden tree. His symbolic act touched off a restoration campaign that between 1948 and 1958 had many men and women hard at work planting the generation of trees that have since grown to splendid maturity.

*Top: "Amazon on Horseback" (Amazone zu Pferd) by Louis Tuaillon seen in the eastern edge of the Tiergarten in 1907. The original version of this sculpture is found in the National Gallery on the Museum Island*

*Middle: Hungry Berliners harvest potatoes next to Tuaillon's Amazon, October 21st, 1947. The harvest was poor that year, with the average potato no larger than the size of a golf ball*

*Bottom: The trees have returned to the Tiergarten in full force. Many of the oldest specimens date back to a British tree-planting campaign launched by the young Princess (now Queen) Elizabeth*

# ST HEDWIG'S CATHEDRAL

In a remarkable gesture of tolerance for a rival faith Frederick the Great, a Calvinist, announced plans for a new church to serve the many Catholics who had migrated to Berlin following his army's successful conquest of Silesia. Named after the protectress of Silesia, St Hedwig's church was the first Catholic house of worship to be built in the city in over 200 years. Plans for the church were based on the king's own sketches, and completed by architect Georg von Knobelsdorff.

The cathedral's construction, begun in 1747, was an interminable affair that went on for almost 150 years. Distracted by his on-going conflict with the Austrians, the king lost interest in the project shortly after it began, forcing his artisans to lay down their tools before the roof could be completed. A decade later, Cardinal Quirini stepped in with the cash necessary to give the cathedral its long-awaited dome, for which he was granted immortality by having his name engraved on the frieze above the cathedral's main entrance.

The king originally intended the completed dome to resemble the famous Pantheon of Rome, although some said the end result looked more like an upside-down tea cup. In any event, the partially-completed church satisfied the monarch's taste for Baroque architecture, a motif that was to become pervasive in the collection of Neo-Classical public buildings to take shape on the Unter den Linden throughout his reign.

More than a century would pass before St Hedwig's large central dome was properly fitted with a protective coat of copper. Shortly thereafter, in 1892, the final component of the church's original plan was carried out when the dome's cupola and cross were at long last installed. Sculptor Nicolaus Geiger provided a finishing touch by executing a relief of the Adoration of the Magi in the front portal's gabled pediment.

*Opposite: The renovated altar in 1930,
the year the church was named as cathedral
to the newly-formed Catholic Diocese
of Berlin*

*Below: St Hedwig's Cathedral on the Opernplatz in 1889,
just two years after the central dome finally received
its cupola and cross. No longer would people accuse the
building of looking like an upside-down tea cup*

When the Catholic Diocese of Berlin was formed in 1930, St Hedwig's Church was named as its cathedral. By then, the old church was in desperate need of repairs. A crudely executed restoration ensued, one that gutted the chapel's decaying interior and replaced it with more simplified surroundings.

During the war, the Catholic Bishop of Berlin, Count Konrad Preysing, regularly held sermons at St Hedwig's Cathedral. A prominent figure among the clerical opposition to Hitler and his policies, Preysing ran a continual risk of provoking charges such as "malice", "misuse of the pulpit" and "treason". Hitler's propaganda chief, Joseph Goebbels, monitored the Bishop's sermons by infiltrating agents of the SD (Security Service) into the congregation but he never moved to arrest the Bishop, preferring to confront him only after the war had been won.

The cathedral was severely damaged during the night of March 1st, 1943, when a swarm of 156 British Lancaster bombers breached city defences.

Rebuilding of St Hedwig's Cathedral commenced under the direction of architect Hans Schwippert in 1952 and took ten years. In 1961, a bland, prefabricated shell of self-supporting concrete slabs was positioned over the chapel, replacing the original dome of wood, stone and copper. Restoration work concluded the following year consisted of a more detailed renovation of the cathedral's interior.

Since July of 1994, the St Hedwig's Cathedral has served as the seat of a re-established Catholic Diocese of Greater Berlin.

*Opposite: "Trümmerfrauen" (rubble women) clear out piles of bricks in front of the church in December 1945*

*Below: The cathedral today. It now serves as the seat of the re-established Catholic Diocese of Greater Berlin*

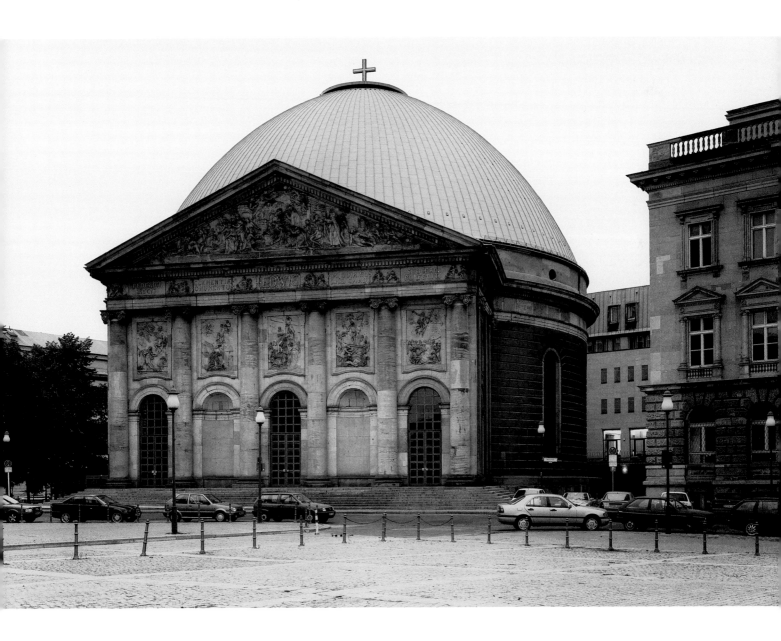

# BERLIN CATHEDRAL

Lack of funds, a revolution and royal indecision delayed the construction of Berlin's most recognised cathedral for much of the 19th century. Finally, after a great deal of soul-searching, Emperor William II approved architect Julius Raschdorff's third set of drawings and funding of 10 million marks from the Prussian parliament was secured. In 1893, work on the "emperor's cathedral" began.

Once the old cathedral that occupied the site was demolished and the royal crypt beneath it readied for the construction work to come, huge blocks of granite and sandstone began arriving from various Silesian quarries by barge. As armies of stonemasons and bricklayers laboured to complete the main cupola, coppersmiths working in ateliers from Saxony to the Harz mountains crafted the copper sheets that would cover the roof. In the north-east corner tower, three ancient bells (the oldest one dating from 1471) were hooked up to an electric mechanism. As a finishing touch, three massive bronze doors designed by the great sculptor Otto Lessing were installed at the cathedral's western entrance. A dozen years and 11.5 million marks later, the structure was complete. The Emperor's delight with his new church was tempered by the fact its completion had been promised to him five years earlier.

Even before the cathedral officially opened its doors in 1905, its elaborate architecture stirred controversy. Contemporary Berliners scorned its "outburst of Prussian rhetoric", while the Baedeker guidebook sniffed at its "excess of plastic ornamentation". Christopher Isherwood later referred to it as the "Church of the Immaculate Consumption".

Nevertheless, the cathedral remained the religious venue of choice for many prominent Berliners. One of its more notable parishioners was none other than Hitler's right hand man, Hermann Göring. The Reichsminister was married here on April 11th, 1935, in a ceremony sanctioned by the Nazi State Church. He and his bride, actress Emmy Sonnemann, entered

*Above left: An early photo of the cathedral's largest chamber, the sermon Church*

*Above right: Reichsminister Hermann Goering and his new bride, actress Emmy Sonnemann, leave the cathedral after their marriage ceremony in the spring of 1935*

Below: The Berlin Cathedral, designed by Julius Raschdorff and completed in 1905. Many found its profusion of spires and pediments a trifle overbearing, but the Emperor was delighted with the result

*Right: Exterior view of the Berlin Cathedral seen from the Lustgarten in July, 1945*

*Above: Divine intervention: a 250-kilo bomb crashed through the main cupola but failed to explode*

*Below: Interior view of the cathedral's sermon church and the gaping hole in the floor left by the 250-kilo "Block Buster" bomb*

the cathedral that day through a canopy of sabres, held aloft by generals of the German army, navy and air force. Gifts of princely tribute were expected — and received — from cities, unions, factories and museums all over Germany. Among the booty was a bullet-proof Mercedes from Daimler-Benz, sapphires from Tsar Boris of Bulgaria, and a complete dinner service of Breslau Castle porcelain from the Reichsbank. As Göring and his bride left the church in a blizzard of flower petals, 200 planes of the newly-formed Luftwaffe flew in formation overhead.

The cathedral's controversial appearance was to be permanently altered during the British aerial bombing campaigns of 1940. Then, on May 24th, 1944, incendiary bombs from yet another air raid set the main dome on fire. The floor of the sermon church was breached, causing pews, beams and chunks of stone to crash through the ground floor and into the royal crypt, damaging some of its wood and pewter coffins. Still more devastation occurred during the great firebombing raid of February 3rd, 1945, which finally brought services to a halt.

Three months after the war, sermons resumed deep in the ruined structure's catacombs, but the cathedral was now in the Soviet sector and, with religious activities in the communist part of Berlin discouraged, the ragged congregation eventually dispersed. Though gutted by fire and pocked with artillery shells, the structure was nevertheless spared the wrecker's ball. The communist city planners felt it would be too expensive to demolish so, after some emergency structural repairs, the cathedral was permitted to stand in silence for the next three decades.

An offer of financing from West German Protestant churches in 1974 prompted the East German Government to finally initiate reconstruction of the cathedral's soot-blackened exterior. As part of its guidelines for the reconstruction of historic buildings, the GDR-based Institute for the Preservation of Historic Monuments called for the "modification or removal of details with strong ideological content". As such, the communist government avoided an exact duplication of the cathedral's Wilhelmine cupolas, choosing instead to erect more anonymous, stylised spires that would arouse less religious sentiment from passers-by. As a result, the structure is now 16 metres shorter than Raschdorff's pre-war version. In the end, the cathedral's reconstruction period outlived the communist regime itself. On June 7th, 1993, Chancellor Helmut Kohl officially opened the newly-restored sermon church to the general public. Administered by the "Evangelische Kirche der Union", the cathedral currently provides a place of worship for Christians from all over Berlin.

*The recently-restored Berlin Cathedral.*
*In the foreground can be seen the*
*reconstructed Lustgarten*

# REICHSBANK

The decision to build a new addition to Germany's ageing Reichsbank headquarters was taken in the last days of the Weimar government, although its design competition opened just weeks after Hitler was elected Chancellor, in January 1933. Ludwig Mies van der Rohe's modernist entry ultimately took first prize, winning out over submissions by Walter Gropius, Heinrich Tessenow and Hans Poelzig.

Despite Mies van der Rohe's imposing façade and sweeping dimensions that included a 350-foot long public hall, Hitler complained that it and all the other proposed designs were not "monumental" enough. The Reichsbank Technical Department took the hint and rejected all the entries. Their own building department chief, Heinrich Wolff, was left to execute the project.

The new complex, just across the street from the old Reichsbank building, was to occupy 13 acres of prime downtown real estate and required the demolition of the old Royal Mint as well as the eradication of two smaller streets. Work on the 40 million mark project started in 1934 and reached completion three years later. Wolff's completed structure of steel-reinforced concrete rose seven storeys high and had an exterior finished in pale sandstone.

Hjalmar Schacht, who moved in to the new building's presidential suite, was no stranger to the pressures of the job. At the height of Germany's hyper-inflation when the mark's worth sank to 3.8 trillion to one US dollar, Schacht had been called upon to implement a scheme which sought to replace the old mark with the new Rentenmark, a unit of currency tied to a national mortgage on Germany's assets. One of the first things he did was put the currency speculators out of business by revoking their lines of credit. He then spent the next month locked in a little office in the old Reichsbank building furiously smoking cigars with one hand and telephoning every financial contact he could think of with the other. Schacht's attempt to persuade key international players of the Rentenmark's value was a stunning success.

As President of the Reichsbank during the Nazi years, Schacht and his officials faced a different challenge: maintaining a healthy national balance sheet while funding a long list of capital-intensive projects, from highway construction to nuclear research.

In the wake of the Wehrmacht's advance across Europe, the national gold reserves of its conquered countries were confiscated and shipped to the Reichsbank vaults where they were held until they could be used to trade with neutral countries for vital war supplies.

In May of 1945, a Russian "trophy brigade" burst into the Reichsbank vaults hoping to get its hands on some of the estimated $621 million the Nazis had looted from Germany's neighbours. All they found, however, was a paltry $3 million in gold bars and a collection of rare musical instruments. Most of the Reichsbank's fortune had already been thrown down mine shafts or deposited in secret bank accounts.

After the war, the new communist masters moved in and de-nazified Wolff's décor, chipping away the huge bas-relief eagles that adorned either side of the main foyer and filing off all the bronze swastikas from the doorknobs. The first tenants of the politically sanitized structure were the East German Finance Ministry, and later, the Central Committee of the East German communist party, the Socialist Unity Party (SED). Later, party chairman Erich Honecker worked out of his offices here until he was eased from his post in the last days of the regime. A spirited debate over the fate of the Reichsbank building followed Bonn's decision

*Opposite: The freshly-scrubbed Reichsbank building today, looking much as it did when it first opened in 1938*

*Below: The northern entrance to the former Reichsbank building in 1960. By then, it was serving as headquarters for East Germany's political élite*

to relocate to Berlin. In the end, the Foreign Ministry reluctantly agreed to occupy the site.

On August 25th, 1996, Berliners were given one last chance to see the luxurious, yet dated offices of the GDR's élite before the renovation crews moved in. Public response to the open house event was overwhelming. Huge crowds flocked to the old Reichsbank building and waited in line for hours for a chance to see the offices and corridors where, not so long ago, their communist leaders had worked. (The Politburo's meeting room, complete with its U-shaped conference table and plush red chairs, have since been preserved, although Honecker's office has not.)

# NEW REICH CHANCELLERY

After coming to power in 1933, Adolf Hitler moved out of the Kaiserhof Hotel and across the street to a building that had served as official residence of Germany's heads of state since the days of Otto von Bismarck. Despite Hitler's euphoria at finally being elected Chancellor, he was less than pleased with the Chancellery's dusty chambers, some of which dated back to 1739.

Hitler immediately ordered renovations to the Chancellery building and had a sizeable new addition tacked onto the back. Then, in 1935, he had his chief architect, Albert Speer, build him a new portico and a balcony on the second floor of the Chancellery overlooking the Wilhelmstrasse. The Führer wanted to be seen from three sides when he gave speeches to his adoring crowds.

On January 10th 1937, Hitler asked his architect to design a new building that would inspire a sense of awe to all those who passed through its marble halls. The new Chancellery had to reflect the virility and strength of purpose of the new Reich. And even though heavy military spending had almost wiped out the Reichsbank's gold reserves, Hitler declared that no expense would be spared in the Chancellery's construction. One year later, Speer had his plans approved and was given the green light to begin construction. Eager to impress his patron, the architect promised that the project would be completed in just 12 month's time.

Over the next year, the Voss Strasse was the scene of frenetic construction activity, where a 4,500-man construction team worked day and night to complete the project. One year later, the completed Chancellery was presented to Hitler, 48 hours ahead of schedule. Its opening, designed to coincide with the annual reception of Berlin's diplomatic community, was inaugurated with a dinner of epic proportions. Three companies of SS and SA men served the crowds of diplomats,

*Above: Hitler greets Italian ambassador Bernardo Attolico in his study. The ambassador had tried his best to initiate last-minute peace negotiations on the eve of World War II, but only managed to irritate Joachim von Ribbentrop and other high-ranking Nazis*

*Opposite below: An imposing view of the new Reich Chancellery as seen looking east on the Voss Strasse in 1939*

*Right: The Führer's inner sanctum, which overlooked the Chancellery gardens. To the left is the spacious map table he would use to plot his conquests*

*Far right: Russian soldiers poke around Hitler's study in 1945*

party functionaries and captains of German industry. The dinner guests were invited to tour a grandiose maze of reception halls and marbled galleries that included over 420 rooms covering a floor space of 360,000 square metres.

A foreign diplomat arriving that evening at the New Chancellery would approach the building through an opening in the Wilhelmstrasse and enter a paved, barren enclosure called the Ehrenhof — the Court of Honour. He would then alight from his vehicle, walk up a stone staircase past two bronze male statues executed by Hitler's favourite sculptor, Arno Breker, and enter a small, rather plain vestibule. From there he would proceed through a pair of 17-foot high doors into a much larger chamber, called the Mosaic Hall. Serving no other purpose other than to impress, this enormous, windowless vault of inlaid marble walls was completely devoid of furniture or carpets.

On the visitor would walk, footsteps echoing hollowly, until he reached yet another chamber, called the Runde Saal. This room, also windowless, was completely round. Overhead, as if seen from the bottom of a well, was a large skylight.

By now the exhausted diplomat would have covered a tenth of a kilometre from his car and he was still less than half way to the Chancellery's reception area. He still had the 146-metre-long Marble Gallery ahead of him. Twice the length of Versailles' Hall of Mirrors and long enough to land a light aircraft on, the corridor was lit on one side with a series of floor-to-ceiling windows and decorated with 17th century tapestries on the other. Each end of the Gallery was deliberately kept in deep shade to add to the sense of limitless depth.

The pink and green marble floors underfoot were always polished and gleaming — there were no carpets. At one point Speer, who was accompanying Hitler through the Marble Gallery, remarked that its smooth floor

*Far left: The Wilhelmstrasse entrance to the Reich Chancellery in 1938. The Chancellery building was built in 1931 just two years before the Nazi rise to power*

*Left: View of the ruined Chancellery in 1946. The portal was added later and leads to the "Court of Honour" of the New Reich Chancellery*

*View of the Chancellery 10 years later. Note the narrow-gauge railway that has been set up on the Voss Strasse looking east in 1949*

British Prime Minister Winston Churchill
emerges from the Führerbunker during his
visit to Berlin in July, 1945

could pose a hazard to visitors. "That's exactly right," replied Hitler.
"Diplomats should have practice moving on a slippery surface."

Half way along the Gallery to the right, the visiting diplomat would
come upon two armed guards standing in front of a set of heavy rose-
wood doors over which, in a bronze scroll, were the overlapped initials,
AH. This was Adolf Hitler's study. If the diplomat had personal business
with the Führer, instead of continuing on to the reception area, the guards
would step aside and the visitor would pass into the dictator's inner sanctum. Crossing a deep, reddish brown carpet, the visitor would perhaps be
given the opportunity to admire the ancient tapestries and bronze medal-
lions that hung on the dictator's walls of blood-red marble. He might be
asked to have a seat in front of a huge fireplace that had an oil painting
of Bismarck hung over the mantelpiece, or if business was more urgent,
he would be shown to Hitler's desk in the north-west corner of the room.
The desk front was inlaid with the heads of Medusa and Athena as well
as a glowering depiction of Mars with his sword half out of its scabbard.
Hitler particularly liked the last one. "...when the diplomats sitting at the
front of my desk see this, they will learn the meaning of dread."

Some of the Chancellery's more extravagant design features were
removed as the effects of a lengthening war made themselves felt. In
1941, all its bronze doors, as well as the radiator screens and other
assorted architectural hardware were removed and melted down to make
artillery shells. However, this was only the beginning of the Chancellery's

transformation. As Berlin fell increasingly vulnerable to Allied air raids, the 1/4 mile-long Nazi headquarters became an obvious and tempting target.

As the air raids worsened, an excavation firm was contracted to deepen and expand Hitler's command bunker under the Chancellery garden. The bunker's roof was bolstered with a 16-foot layer of reinforced concrete, which was in turn covered over with tons of earth. A 90-foot tunnel connected the bunker to the Chancellery basement.

Aboveground, the Reich Chancellery continued to suffer direct hits from the waves of British and American bombers that appeared with increasing regularity over Berlin skies after 1942. Its walls of yellow stucco and grey stone sustained particularly heavy damage on January 28th, 1944, during an air raid that left 180,000 Berliners homeless.

On January 16th, 1945, Hitler returned to Berlin from the south, following the defeat of the Ardennes Offensive. His last desperate attempt to

*Above: The "Court of Honor". Albert Speer had special permission to park his supercharged Horch automobile here*

---

*Above right: The Chancellery's fire-scorched courtyard in the fall of 1945*

forestall the inevitable had failed totally. Barring the sudden appearance of a new wonder weapon, the fate of the "Third Reich" was sealed.

Within hours of his arrival, the dictator and his adjutant, weighed down with a few of Hitler's personal belongings, descended 44 steps into the so-called Führer bunker in the Chancellery garden. Apart from a few brief visits aboveground, Hitler would never see the light of day again.

As the Russians pressed ever closer to Berlin, the Reich Chancellery itself took on a new role.

On April 23rd, 1945, two thousand troops commanded by Major General Wilhelm Mohnke occupied the complex's cavernous basement in preparation for Operation Clausewitz, a futile attempt to make a last stand against the tightening Soviet ring. By then, the Chancellery building was being systematically raked with shellfire from their own deadly 88 twin-purpose guns, which had been trained on them from their captured positions in Tempelhof Airport. "The Red Army's massed artillery was spraying us like conscientious gardeners," said Dr. Ernst-Günther Schenk, who worked inhuman hours trying to patch up the wounded in the Chancellery basement.

On April 30th, 1945, at about 3:30 p.m., with the Russian soldiers just a city block away, an addled, trembling Hitler sat down on a white and blue velvet settee in his cramped quarters 55 feet below street level. He raised the barrel of his black Walther pistol next to his temple and pulled the trigger. This much-anticipated gunshot set off a mad scramble to the bunker exits, as members of his entourage began their hazardous trek north towards the British lines. Some managed to escape the city, most did not.

Two months after the end of the war, Winston Churchill arrived to tour the Chancellery ruins and the dank recesses of Hitler's bunker. Upon his arrival, he was cheered by a crowd of Berliners who had heard the British Prime Minister was scheduled to appear. Their welcome touched Churchill, and he later wrote, "My hate had died with their surrender, and I was much moved by their demonstrations."

The Soviets began demolition of the shell-pocked Chancellery building in 1947. Their East German successors continued this undertaking off and on for the next 18 years. The massive limestone complex was initially an important source of building materials for Soviet monument builders. A narrow-gauge railway was set up to transport some of the stonework to the eastern suburbs where a Soviet war memorial was under construction. Some of the Chancellery marble was also used to line the walls of a subway station and refurbish the Soviet Embassy. The last vestiges of the Chancellery building were finally cleared away in 1965.

For many years a mine-filled no-man's-land that bordered the Berlin Wall, the eastern portion of the Reich Chancellery site is now home to an apartment complex built by the East German communists during the last years of their rule. The remaining land is currently under development.

Sections of the Chancellery bunker system that sheltered Hitler and his staff from Allied bombs and artillery still lie beneath the surface. Part of this dank, subterranean world was accidentally exposed during a tree-planting effort in March of 1990.

Yet another part of the bunker complex was laid bare a few months later in preparation for a rock concert. This second discovery revealed a 10 x 30 metre chamber whose walls still bore vivid frescoes of steel-helmeted soldiers protecting mothers and children from unseen enemies. Ongoing excavations are still uncovering more of these concrete burrows from Germany's dark days. As late as 1997, crews working to lay a road just north of the Chancellery site uncovered a secret bunker believed to have been made for Joseph Goebbels. It is believed even the GDR government was unaware of its existence.

*Above: Albert Speer's Runder Saal, a windowless marble chamber whose prime purpose was to impress and intimidate. And the Runder Saal after its capture by the Russians in 1945. Not only windowless, it was now missing a floor*

*Below: Contemporary view of the Reich Chancellery site looking east on the Voss Strasse. The former Nazi headquarters is now an apartment complex built in the last days of the East German regime*

# AIR MINISTRY

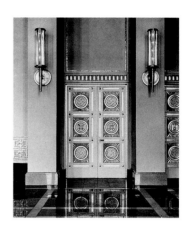

In February 1935, work began on a massive, 2800-room headquarters for Germany's Air Ministry. Part of the complex was intended to house the offices of Germany's civil aviation authority, but its chief purpose was to serve the ballooning bureaucracy of Hermann Göring's newly-formed Luft-waffe.

The gigantic limestone structure was completed in just eight months, with crews working double shifts and on Sundays. Its imposing design was the work of 43-year-old Ernst Sagebiel, an individual who, despite his past association with modernist Erich Mendelsohn, had the ability to mim-ic the Neo-Classical lines favoured by Hitler. Sagebiel was involved in a number of important Nazi-era projects, including the redesign of Tempel-hof Airport.

All those who entered Sagebiel's completed building were exposed to a variety of architectural trickery. From the eerie, backlit entrance hall to the doorknobs that were positioned a few inches above the normal waist height, the goal was to humble and intimidate. Least subtle in this respect was the huge marble "Hall of Honour", where an oversized golden eagle gazed imperiously downward from its elevated position on the oppo-site wall.

Hitler's secretary, Martin Bormann, grumbled about the grandiose dimensions of the ministry, but this was to be just the beginning. Once the war had been won, Göring intended to build himself an even larger complex just south of the Tiergarten.

For the next decade, 4000 bureaucrats and their secretaries would hurry up and down the Air Ministry's seven kilometres of corridors, fever-ishly processing the mountain of paperwork required to manage Hitler's rapidly-growing air force. Although Göring was head of the organisation his deputy Erhard Milch, former head of Lufthansa, remained in charge of day-to-day decision making.

*Opposite: Double bronze doors leading to one of the former air ministry's cavernous reception halls*

*Below: Hermann Göring's massive Reich Air Ministry building on 81–85 Wilhelmstrasse*

Below: The southern wing of the Air Ministry somewhat the worse for wear in July of 1945. The Soviet Military Administration (SMAD) occupied this building for the next four years

Ernst Sagebiel's buildings seemed to lead charmed lives because, like Tempelhof Airport, the huge Air Ministry building survived the war almost completely intact. This, in a neighbourhood that had 92 percent of its structures destroyed by aerial bombardment. Part of the building's feat of survival could be attributed to its upper floor ceilings, which were topped with 60 cm of steel-reinforced concrete.

Once the dust had settled in May, 1945, the former Air Ministry found itself just inside the Russian zone. It was initially occupied by the Soviet Military Administration (SMAD) but in 1949, the Russian-sponsored regime headed by Wilhelm Pieck invaded the damaged complex with its own army of bureaucrats and functionaries. From within these bullet-scarred walls, the founding of the GDR was proclaimed to the world.

During the early years of the communist regime, the former Air Ministry became home to the GDR's Economic Council. Later, as more governmental departments moved in, the complex was known by its Orwellian name, the "House of Ministries". In an effort to liven up its grim exterior, fourteen artisans from the Meissen porcelain works were hired to complete a large fresco on the north-east corner entrance in early 1952. The result was a picture of socialist harmony, complete with a farmhand sharing a laugh with a truck driver and two accordion players leading a phalanx of blue-shirted women off into the sunset. The mural's tiles, some of which have since gone a milky white, still adorn the building's corner entrance.

In June of the following year, three hundred construction workers gathered in front of the House of Ministries to protest at an increase to their production quotas. The angry mob quickly grew in number to 5,000 as more East Berliners joined in the protest. Fearing a full-scale civil revolt, the SED government threw up barricades in front of the Ministry doors and called on the Soviets to help them deal with the "anti-social"

*Assembly in the Hall of Honour of the Reich Air Ministry at the time of National Socialism*

elements who threatened to storm the building. The Russians responded with T-34 tanks and machine guns. By the end of the following day the revolt had been brutally snuffed out, at a cost of 360 lives. In response to that bleak day, the West German government changed the name of the boulevard that bisects the Tiergarten the Strasse des 17. Juni.

Being on the very edge of the boundary that separated East and West Berlin, the old Air Ministry building had a new neighbour in 1961 — the Berlin Wall. This grotesque attempt to divide the city led to a spectacular escape from Göring's former headquarters four years later when a resourceful elevator repairman managed to gain access to the building's rooftop.

The escapee attached a steel cable to a support beam on the roof's surface and, with the help of some students on the western side, connected the cable to another anchoring point on the other side of the Wall. Later that evening, the students managed to short-circuit several arc lights that lit up that portion of the border and helped the repairman and two family members slide down the cable on a steel harness to the American sector.

After unification, the legions of state functionaries of the former GDR vacated their offices to make way for employees of the Treuhandanstalt, an enormous holding company set up by the government of Chancellor Helmut Kohl to sell the real estate and commercial assets held by the defunct East German regime. Its first director, Detlev Rohwedder, was brutally murdered, presumably, by the Red Army Fraction in 1991. The complex since then goes by the name Detlev Rohwedder Building in honour of the slain former head of the Treuhand.

Within a period of five years the agency managed to liquidate most of the items in its 600-page catalogue of state-owned enterprises, from hair salons to shipyards.

Initially, when the German government decided to move to Berlin, it rejected the idea that any of its ministries would be housed in Nazi-era structures like the former Air Ministry building. Bonn preferred to demolish these tainted relics and replace them with shining new ministries of its own. This plan, however, encountered widespread resistance among a large number of preservationists of all political colours in Berlin. A report commissioned by the city government stated, "There are alternatives more appropriate to the culture of Berlin and the Federal Republic of Germany than simply disposing of history by tearing down buildings." Others pointed out that if the Soviets found it acceptable to occupy the Tsarist Kremlin, then Germany's foreign ministry could just as easily occupy the Reichsbank building.

In the end, these arguments plus the staggering cost of reconstruction persuaded Bonn to reconsider its position and announce that the former

The southern wing of the newly renamed "House of Ministries" during the June 1953 Uprising. Soviet tanks and troops had assembled to crush a workers' revolt against the increasingly unpopular East German regime

Air Ministry would be in fact be converted for government use. As faint consolation, it was recalled that the building had once sheltered the activities of the "Red Orchestra" resistance movement that tried to overthrow Adolf Hitler.

The Federal Finance Ministry subsequently offered to occupy the rundown premises only recently occupied by East Germany's top ministers, but not without some reservations. One senior official who inspected the building described its condition as "dreadful", adding, "I asked myself if it were thinkable that the ruling class of an industrial nation would use such toilets."

The architectural firm HPP won the contract to modernise the protected landmark, at a staggering cost of 300 million DM. This high cost reflected the scope of the work to be done. Virtually everything needed to be replaced, from the building's worn elevator cables to its antique sprinkler systems. Over 4,000 windows needed to be replaced, and the entire soot-blackened limestone exterior required a good scrubbing.

Shortly after the clean-up began, restoration supervisor Wolfgang Keilholz faced a delicate situation. He suspected that the Soviets, in their post-war effort to "de-nazify" the building, did not destroy all the fascist symbology that adorned the building's limestone façade and simply reversed its exterior stone panels.

Preferring to let sleeping dogs lie, Keilholz chose to clean the panels with more superficial techniques rather than dismantle the walls for a more thorough restoration. A second dilemma arose when a Nazi-era time capsule was discovered as crews were restoring the basement foundations. After some consultation, the decision was taken to catalogue the container's contents and seal it back into the foundation for future generations to discover.

The former Air Ministry's once-desolate courtyards have now been softened by greenery, and its decrepit GDR-era interior now hums with the latest in building technology.

In the end, the new Detlev Rohwedder Building has managed to strike a delicate balance between respecting history and serving the needs of a modern, democratic government.

*While its exterior appears virtually unchanged, Göring's air ministry*
*building has undergone a thorough makeover inside*

# TEMPELHOF AIRPORT

On August 30th, 1909, residents in Berlin's southern district of Tempelhof spotted a strange object hovering overhead. This apparition turned out to be the work of Graf von Zeppelin; he had just arrived from Lake Constance in his Z6 airship and was paying a visit to Berlin to demonstrate his wonderful new invention. At 12:50 p.m. that day, he lifted off from Tempelhof's parade grounds and floated towards the Imperial Palace. After making a wide, lazy circuit over the City Hall (Rathaus) and Petrikirche, he swung back over Unter den Linden, continued over Moabit, and docked at the Tegel artillery range where an excited emperor waited to greet him. Von Zeppelin's airship was not the only bizarre craft to appear over Berlin skies that summer. Just one week later, the Tempelhof parade grounds hosted Berlin's first air race. American aviators Orville and Wilbur Wright were among those lured here by a 150,000-mark purse put up by a local newspaper for the aviator who could make it between Tempelhof and Johannesthal in the fastest time. The Americans lost to an Englishman by the name of Hubert Latham who, besides taking home the winnings, was issued a ticket by Berlin authorities for gross mischief.

*Above left: Passengers patiently wait for the next flight out, circa 1935*

*Above: Architect Ernst Sagebiel (left) inspects a scale model of the airport project*

*Left: One of Graf Zeppelin's airships pays Berlin a visit at Tempelhof in May, 1931*

102

*Below: Close-up view of Sagebiel's enormous model.*
*Only a fraction of his planned complex was ever built*

*Allied bombs fall from the sky in February, 1945.*
*The airport, bottom left, somehow managed to survive the war intact*

*Right: An American C-47 transport plane flies over Tempelhof during the Berlin Airlift*

Before long, more and more wood and canvas flying machines could be seen taking off like awkward dragonflies out of Tempelhof's fields. Then in 1924, a small shed was built to shelter the few intrepid air travellers who actually paid to ride in these contraptions. Within a few years, more robust aircraft were making their presence felt in the skies over Berlin. In 1926, Deutsche Lufthansa formed out of several smaller airlines and started to provide regular mail service and passenger flights to destinations across Europe.

Tempelhof's original passenger shed was expanded several times to accommodate increased air traffic, but in 1936 work began on a vast new project that would transform the terminal into a world-class airport. The architect for this mammoth undertaking was Ernst Sagebiel, the same person who designed Hermann Göring's Air Ministry building on the Leipziger Strasse. His plans called for an enormous curved canopy that would allow passengers to disembark from the planes and proceed directly into the terminal without ever being exposed to the elements.

Even though the structure was still under construction in 1938, it had already become the busiest airport in central Europe. Over 247,000 passengers on 63,000 flights passed though its terminal that year. Although overseas flights were still a rarity, Tempelhof nonetheless offered its travellers a choice of direct flights to 43 international destinations.

During the war, Tempelhof Airport had great strategic value and as such it was defended to the teeth by the heavily-armed SS Nordland Tank Division. In its headlong rush to capture the capital, the advancing Red Army simply bypassed the airport with its tanks and pressed on to the Reich Chancellery. The German defenders remained trapped in the airport while the battle ranged on around them. Incredibly, Lufthansa was still using Tempelhof for its commercial flights while all this was going on.

On April 21st, 1945, less than ten days before the fall of Berlin, its last plane left Tempelhof with nine passengers bound for Stockholm. The airline would not return to Berlin for another 45 years.

In spring of 1945, the airport briefly served as a base for the Soviet air force, but on July 4th of that year it was handed over to the U.S. armed forces as per the Yalta accords. This wartime agreement stated that Berlin would be administered jointly by the four Allied powers in a spirit of amicable co-operation, but events would prove otherwise.

After three years of deteriorating relations, the Soviet Union attempted to rid itself of the British, French and American presence in Berlin by trying to starve their sectors into submission. In the spring of 1948, it abruptly severed all road and rail links to West Berlin. But rather than abandon this awkward piece of ruined real estate deep in the Russian Zone, the Western allies made a commitment to supply their half of Berlin by air. It was a gamble that many thought was doomed to failure.

As the airlift got underway, Tempelhof Airport became the scene of incredible activity. On June 25th, 1948, the first C-47 transport plane landed here, loaded with freeze-dried food and coal. As the campaign geared up, more and more planes arrived with vital supplies. At its height, one plane every 22 seconds touched down on the airport's runway. Each pilot had only one chance to land. If no landing was possible, he had to return to the west and wait to be assigned another place in line. By the time the airlift ended, millions of tons of essential goods, including the components for an entire electrical generating station, had been flown in.

In due course, the Soviets realised that their pressure tactics was making heroes out of their enemies. On May 12th, 1949, they reluctantly lifted their blockade.

Throughout the early Cold War years, civilian air traffic continued to flow though Tempelhof's terminus although the communist regime forbade all but British, French and American airlines from using any of the three air corridors that passed over GDR territory. (Only after unification could airlines like Lufthansa resume their flights to Berlin.)

By 1959, air traffic to West Berlin had increased to the point where Tempelhof, as West Berlin's busiest airport, was reaching its maximum capacity. Because no further expansion was possible in this heavily-populated area, the smaller Tegel airfield in the French sector was selected for future development. In 1975, civilian flights were transferred to Tegel's newly-expanded facilities. The US Air Force continued to use Tempelhof until their final departure in 1994.

As one of the world's oldest airports, Tempelhof remains very much in use today as a transit point for short-haul flights from across Germany and Europe. The terminal, which is approaching its ninth decade of operation, handles over a million passengers per year.

*Right: Soviet troops admire the view of Berlin from the passenger terminal roof in May, 1945*

*Below: Tempelhof's passenger terminal today. The eagle seen in the 1945 photo stood above its main entrance until the 1960s, when it was removed to make way for radar equipment*

# HOUSE OF TOURISM

The office block that briefly stood on the north side of the Potsdam Bridge was an abortive beginning to a Nazi reconstruction plan of staggering proportions. Had the war not intervened, it would have been one of the largest engineering projects of the 20th century.

The House of Tourism was intended to occupy the south-west corner of an enormous traffic circle called Runder Platz, modelled after the Place de la Concorde in Paris. The circle itself was to lie directly in the path of a 7-kilometre long boulevard of gargantuan government buildings and head offices of German corporations stretching from a great railway terminus north of the River Spree to another equally sizeable terminus south of Tempelhof Airfield. The end of this "Boulevard of Honour" (Pracht Allee) was to be the People's Great Hall (Volkshalle), a gigantic assembly hall slated for completion by 1950, at which time Hitler planned to host an international exhibition to show off his architectural monstrosities. By then, Berlin was to be called Germania, a name that Hitler felt better reflected the city as the nexus of Teutonic power.

The design and execution of this ambitious project was left to Hitler's chief architect, the 33-year-old Inspector-General of Construction, Albert Speer. Even though it would require vast amounts of cash — 96 billion Reichmarks by some estimates — the project was to proceed at all costs. When Speer informed Hitler that his master plan required the destruction of Dr. Fahrenkamp's Shell Building, St Matthew's Church, several embassies and 50,000 apartments south of the Tiergarten, the Führer did not bat an eye.

In 1938, extensive tracts of prime commercial and residential land were expropriated in preparation for the massive construction project to come. The first building to go up was the House of Tourism. Its founda-

*Right above: The completed House of Tourism, July 1941. By then, the "Germania" project had been shelved, due to a wartime shortage of construction materials*

*Right below: The House of Tourism was the scene of heavy fighting during the Battle for Berlin. This November 1945 photo shows the result. The damaged iron railings of the Potsdam Bridge appear in the foreground*

*Opposite above: Laying of the building's foundation stone, June 14th, 1938*

*Opposite below: Craftsmen put the finishing touches on a gigantic scale model of the House of Tourism.
This project marked the beginning of Hitler's master plan to transform the city into a world capital, to be renamed "Germania"*

tion stone was laid by Hitler in a ceremony held on June 14th of that year, the day ground was broken on sixteen construction sites nearby.

The House of Tourism was completed in the fall of 1941, but shortly thereafter, work on the adjoining complex came to a full stop. The country was at war and precious building materials had to be diverted to other more strategic projects. Speer's master plan would never move forward, although Hitler refused to admit this until the Russians were virtually at his doorstep.

Since this area of south-central Berlin was once the administrative hub of the Third Reich, not much of anything escaped being pounded into brickdust by the waves of British and American bombers which regularly tormented the city between the years 1943-45. But against great odds, the House of Tourism's sturdy frame survived long enough to play a dramatic part in Berlin's last days of the war.

On April 27th, 1945, soldiers of Marshal Chuikov's 2nd Byelorussian Army stood on the southern bank of the Landwehr Canal. They needed to use the Potsdam Bridge directly in front of the House of Tourism to cross the canal and continue their fight north towards the Reich Chancellery. Facing them on the other side of the water were troops commanded by General Karl Weidling, the Commandant of Berlin who had the thankless task of trying to repel the Soviets until a separate peace with the Americans and British could be arranged. He had the bridge mined with explosives, placed some of his men in the House of Tourism and ordered them to pour deadly machine gun fire at anyone who attempted to cross the bridge.

At first, the Russians tried to reach the other side of the canal by passing underground through a subway tunnel, but were beaten back. They then tried a different tactic. A few tanks were covered in diesel-soaked sandbags, set on fire, then driven cross the bridge. The defenders in the House of Tourism saw the blazing tanks approach and were tricked into believing them as destroyed. For a moment, they held their fire, preferring to conserve their precious ammunition for undamaged targets. To their astonishment, the tanks crossed the bridge and started firing on them at close range. This ingenious ruse helped the Russians secure a bridgehead across the Landwehr Canal and open the road to Hitler's bunker which lay just a few blocks away.

In the 1960s, the House of Tourism's crumbling walls were pulled down to make room for the New National Gallery designed by Ludwig Mies van der Rohe.

Today, nothing remains of the House of Tourism and the original Potsdam Bridge. The only clue that tells us where the bridge once stood is the row of alcoves that line the walls of the Landwehr Canal. They served as footings for the span's iron beams

# ZOO FLAK TOWER

In the early hours of August 26th, 1940, a wave of 50 Hampden and Wellington bombers from the British Royal Air Force entered Berlin airspace. Due to heavy cloud cover, the pilots lost their bearings and released most of their armament on farmer's fields well south of the city. As a result, the only part of Berlin to be bombed out in the raid was a wooden garden shack in Rosenthal.

The raid came as a nasty surprise to Nazi leadership. This was the first Allied air raid on Berlin, a city that was supposed to be immune from attack. The event prompted Hitler to sign an order two weeks later, authorizing the construction of six flak towers that would form the backbone of Berlin's air defence system. The towers were to have radar capability, searchlights, flak batteries and a set of heavy long-range guns.

Flak Tower I, a concrete monstrosity that went up in the south-west corner of the Tiergarten, was the first fortification to be pressed into service. Mounted on each corner of the tower's roof were four sets of gigantic naval guns. They were supplied by specially-designed elevators that hauled racks of 120 mm shells up from the depths of the munitions bunker below. When fired, the guns would produce a tremendous roar that threatened to shatter windows for blocks around.

Beneath the guns on the top floor were quarters for the 100 gunners required to man the tower's artillery. The next floor down housed a 95-bed hospital, complete with operating theatres and X-ray rooms. The third level served as a storage area for the coin collection of the

*View of the Zoo Flak Tower looking north across the Landwehr Canal in 1945. These colossal fortifications were called Ordensburgen, or Order Castles, and were intended to protect Berlin from enemy air attack*

former emperor and other national treasures, while a public air raid shelter, storerooms, and kitchens occupied the first two floors. The tower's underground levels were reserved for its air conditioning equipment, power generators, and munitions. The entire complex was completely self-sufficient. It had its own water supply, power generator and enough food to keep a staff of combatants supplied for an entire year.

At the height of hostilities, the fortification sheltered 29,000 civilians and 2,000 combatants. Joseph Goebbels had a few rooms reserved here as an alternative to his secret bunker on the Wilhelmstrasse. In the last days of the war, members of the 18th Panzergrenadier Division continued to occupy the all-but-impregnable tower. Outnumbered by a ratio of 10:1, the defenders ultimately surrendered on May 1st, 1945.

Once peace had returned to the devastated city, the question was, what to do with this enormous hunk of concrete? In light of Berlin's acute building shortage, the tower was briefly pressed into service as a hospital. This was only a temporary measure however; clearly, the eyesore would have to go.

An initial attempt in 1947 by British sappers to dispatch the tower with 20 tons of TNT ended in failure. A few more experiments with beehive charges brought equally disappointing results. The Royal Engineers ultimately settled on a new approach using thermite charges in which 435 holes were drilled into the tower's walls. The resulting explosion which produced enough heat to melt concrete, was a success. The last of the flak tower ruins was cleared away in 1955, to make way for a planned extension of the U-Bahn.

Today, the Zoo Flak Tower site is occupied by the animal enclosures and walkways of the expanded Berlin Zoological Gardens.

*Far left: Kitchen workers pose behind the Zoo Tower's huge stock pots. The tower had enough food to supply its defending troops for one full year*

*Left: Patients languish in the flak tower's air raid shelter. The fortification briefly served as a hospital after the war*

*Above right: For months on end, the flak tower resisted repeated attempts by the British to blow it up. This photo shows the demolished structure in 1948*

*Below right: The flak tower site, now part of the Berlin Zoo, is currently inhabited by wild pigs*

# WIRTSHAUS ALT BERLIN

Today, without a surveyor's rod and a few lucky guesses, it would be almost impossible to determine where the exact site of the "Wirtshaus Alt Berlin" lies; the historic inn and its surrounding neighbourhood has vanished without a trace.

The street corner itself dated back to the mid-13th century when this part of Berlin was a small but growing community of boathands, fishermen and traders known as the Fischerkiez. The old inn and tavern was built roughly 400 years later, just as the city was beginning to show signs of recovery from the devastating effects of the Thirty Years' War.

Disastrous fires, military occupation and plague had laid waste to the old fishermen's quarter between 1628 and 1641. However, the Peace of Westphalia concluded a few years later finally gave Berlin's ruling prince, Frederick William, the breathing room to rebuild. Thanks to his efforts, the nearby docks were restored and the new canal system linking the River Oder and River Elbe was dug. Suddenly, Berlin became the centre of inland trade between Hamburg and the Low Countries and the eastern territories of Silesia and Bohemia. Locally, this meant a sharp increase in river traffic and a rebirth of the neighbourhood.

Despite the efforts of several energetic Hohenzollern princes who succeeded Frederick William, life in the dark and narrow streets around the "Wirtshaus Alt Berlin" was slow to improve. While the Unter den Linden just a few streets north blossomed with Baroque palaces and fashionably-attired nobility, life, even for the middle class here on the corner of Petristrasse, remained simple. Homes were poorly furnished, cold and damp. Food was bland and unhealthy; sanitation was primitive. The regulars who wandered into the tavern for a sociable drink after a long exhausting day would continue to follow a pattern of life almost unchanged for the next 200 years. Only after the effects of the Industrial Revolution finally worked their way into this ancient district early in the

*Opposite: A guide describes the rich history of the old district, circa 1928*

---

*Above right: A quiet corner in the "Fischerkiez", a centuries-old neighbourhood that began as a trading post on the southern edge of the Spree Island. Despite its obvious age, "Wirtshaus Alt Berlin" was not the oldest building in the area. This distinction fell to an even older inn around the corner, called "Zum Nussbaum", which dated back to 1571*

*Right: The devastated tavern and inn at the end of the war. The entire neighbourhood was ultimately levelled to make way for a series of high-rise apartments, many of which became occupied by members of the communist élite*

20th century did locals benefit from such amenities as indoor plumbing and electric light.

It is likely the old tavern's wood and plaster walls went up in flames on the morning of February 3rd, 1945, when a thousand American Flying Fortress and Liberator bombers dropped 2,267 tons of explosives over the central parts of the city. It was the first daylight raid launched by the American air force but it would not be the last.

After the end of World War II, communist city planners felt that any attempt to recreate the area's historic charm was not worth the effort. "It is not our intention to restore the capitalistic city centre," proclaimed the East Berlin chief architect in 1967. The anticipated costs would be "out of all proportion to the attainable effect."

Instead, city planners chose to populate the devastated area with a forest of prefabricated high-rises, creating a high-density neighbourhood that would help to alleviate East Berlin's chronic housing shortage. In 1969, a 21-storey apartment block opened its doors roughly on the spot where the old inn used to stand. It would be the first of seven towers to dominate the area and ultimately shelter a community of 3000 residents.

Many of the fortunate citizens who moved into these brand-new apartments were members of the GDR élite. One such tenant was Markus Wolf, enigmatic head of the Stasi. But regardless of rank, no one was permitted to occupy a unit larger than 75 square metres. A typical apartment covered 29 square metres and consisted of a tiny, windowless bathroom, a narrow kitchen, a small living room and an equally small bedroom. Not a single room in the entire complex was larger than 18 square metres, but each apartment did have central heating and hot water — the epitome of luxury in the East Berlin of the 1960s.

The inhabitants of these high-rises were organised into a highly-structured building co-operative, where "floor groups", "tenants organisations" and "building residents management committees" met regularly to deal with day-to-day tasks. Each floor had a warden to maintain order and each tower had its own bookkeeper to keep track of expenses.

When the time came for a little relaxation, men would don their dinner jackets, women would slip on their best dress and they would all meet for a sociable beer in the tower's club room. Today, this spirit of comradeship lives on. Hundreds of tenants have maintained their membership of the GDR-era "Volkssolidarität", a senior citizens' group that organises day trips and tea socials. They were out in force during their building's 30th anniversary celebration, held in June of 1999.

*Socialist-era apartment blocks*
*now dominate the neighbourhood*
*where the old inn once stood*

# CAFÉ KRANZLER

In 1825, Georg Kranzler, a young sugar baker from Vienna opened a coffee house where the Friedrichstrasse met the grandest boulevard in all of Prussia, the Unter den Linden.

In a bid to attract customers, Herr Kranzler provided smoking salons in his establishment, an inspired idea given that smoking outdoors on the street and in public squares was forbidden at the time. Kranzler also introduced Berlin's first sidewalk terrace, a feature that initially met with strong opposition from city authorities, but one that was quickly adopted by other restauranteurs.

Cafés at the time of Kranzler's founding were convenient places for politically active citizens to gather. Here, they could meet out of earshot of the king's spies to discuss politics or read foreign newspapers that contained accounts of events not reported by Berlin's two heavily censored dailies. Kranzler, however, was different. It was a conservative establishment, frequented by equally conservative customers. Ernst Dronke, an associate of Karl Marx, complained that the atmosphere at Kranzler was hopelessly banal. He was undoubtedly commenting on the crowds of young men who lounged on the café terrace all afternoon eating ice-cream and talking about their horses. Many of these layabouts

*Above: Kranzler's terrace on a fine summer day*

*Right: Café Kranzler on the corner of the Friedrichstrasse and Unter den Linden, 1922. Kranzler's arch rival, Café Bauer, can be seen to the left*

The ruined café as it appeared in November, 1945.
Kranzler temporarily reopened across the street, but eventually
moved its flagship café across town to the Kurfürstendamm

wore military uniforms, which prompted author Friedrich Sass to call Kranzler "the Valhalla of Berlin's officer corps."

By day, business was conducted according to the Kranzler family's strict Austrian ethic (they refused to serve beer or spirits of any kind), but as the shadows lengthened they had to abandon their corner of the street to the masses of hookers who swarmed down the Unter den Linden. In 1892, the concentration of prostitutes in the area had become so heavy, city officials had the police seal off the boulevard after dark. By the 1920s, Berlin's nightlife had migrated north towards the Friedrichstrasse railway station and west to the Kurfürstendamm, allowing the patrons of Kranzler once again to sip their coffee and nibble their cream buns in peace.

Kranzler continued to serve its clients throughout most of World War II, although its coffee was now ersatz and the selection of international newspapers in the smoking room was less than inspiring. By 1941, the cigarette girl had nothing left to sell, so she spent her time sewing up the café's threadbare furniture with parcel string. As the war ground on, the café crowd started to dwindle. The corps of waiters was eventually reduced to three men, all over 70 years old.

When the Red Army smashed its way down the Unter den Linden in May of 1945, the historic café lay in ruins, consumed by one of the hundreds of fires which raged through the stricken city during the last days of the war. After peace had finally returned to Berlin, the owners salvaged what they could out of the rubble and moved the old café across the street. But their efforts at restoring a past life were doomed. Coffee, Kranzler's main commodity, was now extraordinarily difficult to obtain — a pound of coffee beans traded on the black market for 20 litres of gasoline. Furthermore, Soviet efforts at restricting free enterprise in their sector of the city meant that a commercial revival of the Unter den Linden was not likely. Indeed, the heavily damaged Unter den Linden remained in darkness every evening for many years after the war. Street lighting was only restored in 1954. Given this unpromising situation, the owners of Café Kranzler joined the commercial remnants of eastern and central Berlin in their flight to the more friendly British, French and American sectors. In 1957, they opened a new 450-seat café on the corner of the increasingly prosperous Kurfürstendamm and Joachimstaler Strasse. Its red and white awnings and distinctive rotunda on the third floor soon became a familiar West Berlin landmark.

Back in East Berlin, the ruins of the original café were eventually cleared away and replaced with a nondescript Soviet-era office block that housed offices of the nationalised Meissen porcelain manufacturer. This building was in turn demolished in the mid-1980s to make way for the Grand Hotel, a luxury hotel owned by the state-controlled Interhotel group that was meant to attract desperately-needed hard currency.

Inaugurated on August 1st, 1987, the hotel's sandstone facing emulated a classical early 19th century look, a refreshing change from the ill-conceived monstrosities that typified the GDR era. The hotel's interior hall was decorated in a pleasing Art Nouveau motif and its suites at 3,800 marks a night were so opulently furnished that guests could be forgiven if they momentarily forgot they were sleeping in the heart of a communist capital. Recently, Westin Hotels & Resorts signed an agreement to manage the Grand Hotel Maritim until 2017.

Meanwhile back on the Kurfürstendamm, Café Kranzler is living on borrowed time, a victim of the fast-paced world in which we live. Says its manager Dieter Essling on the thinning crowds who now visit the café, "The days in which one killed a couple of hours over a cup of mocha and a newspaper are a thing of the past." Kranzler's 174 years of serving up coffee is due to come to an end in June of 2000 at the latest, when its trademark rotunda is to be turned into a cocktail bar.

*Opposite: A line of cars drives past "Kranzler's Corner" in 1986. In the foreground are the austere offices of the nationalised Meissen Porcelain Works. Directly behind it is the Grand Hotel, still under construction*

*Below: Today, the refurbished Grand Hotel (now the Westin Grand) has expanded to occupy Kranzler's historic street corner*

# PSCHORR HAUS

The Pschorr Haus was one of a dozen great wine and beer houses that made the Potsdamer Platz a magnet for thirsty Berliners throughout the Roaring Twenties. But the tradition of providing food and drink on this south-west corner of the square can be traced back to a much earlier time, when the Potsdamer Platz was still a rural fringe on the west side of the old city customs wall.

Starting around the mid-18th century, French Huguenot colonists fleeing religious persecution in France arrived in this area and started to cultivate local fields. To supplement their incomes, they would offer coffee, baked goods and other simple fare from their homes to city dwellers who passed through the Leipzig Gate on their way to the Tiergarten's open spaces.

In the years that followed, more permanent restaurants and cafés opened on the square to serve the growing neighbourhood of millionaires' villas and country homes that were starting to spread south and west. Leafy retreats like Café Josty on the Potsdamer Platz became a popular place for Berlin's leisure classes to stop and spend a pleasant few hours with friends over a cup of mocha.

Even by the late 19th century, when the square's massive metropolitan hotels had started to dominate the street, a few cafés from a quieter

*Above: The outdated Telschow patisserie in 1909, just months before it was knocked down to make way for the Pschorr Haus*

*Right: A picturesque view of the Pschorr Haus taken from the Potsdam Gate across the Leipziger Platz in 1928*

time stubbornly remained. The Telschow patisserie was one such place. It was a plain, three-storey stone building fronted by a large terrace with a few trees for shade. But the serenity of the terrace was increasingly interrupted as the level of noise and exhaust fumes on the Potsdamer Platz grew. Inevitably, the owners of the Telschow sold their outdated building, and in April of 1909 construction of the Pschorr Haus, an establishment more in keeping with the times began.

The Pschorr Haus was just one of many cavernous wine and beer halls to take root in and around the Potsdamer Platz at the turn of the century. Like the neighbouring Bierhaus Siechen, Weinhaus Huth, and Rheingold, Pschorr Haus represented commercial interests which sought to cater for the pleasure of Berliners on a massive scale. It tried to outdo its competitors with a huge, lavishly decorated hall of carved wood, fine marble and elaborate mosaics. The intended goal was to elevate the act of drinking in public to a more respectable level, while maintaining prices that the masses of new wage earners could nonetheless afford.

The reputation of the Pschorr Haus suffered with the onset of World War II. By 1941, the meals served up by its kitchens had become positively foul. Howard K. Smith, a CBS correspondent who was one

*Above: View of the abandoned Pschorr Haus in 1951. The structure stood just inside the Western zones of occupation, where the British, American and Soviet sectors converged*

*Right: Post-war view of the ruined beer palace. To the left can be seen the Potsdam Gate*

of the last Americans living in Berlin before the USA entered the war, recalled his visit to the Pschorr Haus in the fall of that year. The first thing that struck him as he walked into the restaurant was the reek of bad fish. He sat down at one of the café's white wooden tables and ordered the only meat dish on the menu, which turned out to be "two little sausages of uncertain contents, each about the size of a cigar butt." The tomato soup that came with the meal was equally suspect, described by Smith's companion as "IG Farben paint formula 20-X." Surrounding him were waiting travellers from the neighbouring Potsdam railway station.

Unfortunately, the Pschorr Haus did not survive the war. It likely met its fate sometime between 1943 and 1945 during one of the many Allied air raids that sought to demolish the nearby government buildings on the Wilhelmstrasse. Of the dozen or so beer and wine houses that operated around the Potsdamer Platz, just a single one was left standing. The Weinhaus Huth remained for many years a solitary presence in a vast expanse of brick dust and weeds on the western side of the Berlin Wall.

After the historic events of November 1989, Daimler-Benz (now DaimlerChrysler) seized the opportunity to be the first to develop this once-forgotten part of West Berlin, which had overnight become one of the hottest commercial properties in Europe. The company launched a design competition that ultimately awarded a commission to Italian architect Renzo Piano. His project would be just one component of an "urban district" of interconnected buildings that would extend as far as the Landwehr Canal to the south and the National Library to the west. The gigantic 500,000 square-metre complex includes a hotel, a conference centre, a casino, several theatres, residential space, an indoor mall and offices for the DaimlerChrysler corporate headquarters.

One of the assignments handed to Piano and his team of architects was the design of an 18-storey commercial and retail tower on the edge of the Potsdamer Platz where the Pschorr Haus once stood.

Shortly after excavation of the site began in 1994, work crews began to uncover a number of interesting relics from the square's recent past. Among the strata of brick chips and rusty pipes was a set of intact coffee cups bearing the initials of the long-departed Café Josty, an enamel plate advertising a detective agency on the Potsdamer Strasse, a multiple rocket launcher and the wooden lid of a Schultheiss beer barrel.

The first stage of the $2.4 billion Daimler Benz project opened in the fall of 1998. At the opening ceremony, Renzo Piano called the project "the most extraordinary experience of my life." The tower that now occupies the site of the Pschorr Haus was completed one year later in 1999.

*Opposite: Twin towers of the DaimlerChrysler complex now loom over the Potsdamer Platz. The building to the left occupies the street corner where the Pschorr Haus once stood*

# ROMANISCHES CAFÉ

The Romanisches Café was, in the words of Otto Friedrich, "a great barn of a place" that, in the years since its opening in 1895, became a refuge for artists, radicals and others who sought escape from the self-important bombast of Second Reich society.

Berlin's Bohemian set originally passed their days at the Café des Westens nearby, but a key group of élite artists abandoned the place after the owner moved their reserved table to a less-desirable location in the salon. After sampling a few other establishments in the area, they eventually adopted the Romanisches Café on the Breitscheid Platz. Others followed and for the next several decades, the west end café became the gathering place for Berlin's intelligentsia.

The crowds at the café were physically divided into two distinct groups, known as "pools". One pool was reserved for swimmers, those who had already made a name for themselves in society. The other was a holding tank for the rest of humanity, the unknowns who had yet to make their mark. Swimmers at the café included the painters Dix, Mopp, Krauskopf and Lederer, who amused themselves by scrawling caricatures on paper napkins. Their colleague, Emil Orlik, was known for drawing sketches of people on scraps of paper from inside his pants pocket. At another table, poet and multiple-divorcee Else Lasker-Schüler would hold court with her fabulous friends while a porter called Neitz made sure the crowds of admiring nobodies did not intrude.

Those who languished in the holding tank were no less colourful. Talmudic scholars and Prussian estate owners rubbed shoulders with Marxists in cowboy boots and poets with shoulder-length hair. One mathematician dressed in white wore a monocle and ate earthworms at his table. The poorer patrons in this group practised the classic art of "Nassauerei", which involved nursing a single cup of coffee for as long as they possibly could before they were obliged to either leave or buy another cup.

*Opposite far left:*
*Rendezvous at the Romanisches Café.*
*Regulars were known as "Luftmenschen",*
*people who thrived on café*
*atmosphere*

*Opposite left: A tired waiter makes his*
*final tally at 3 a.m.*

*Above right: The cavernous Romanisches*
*Café in 1931*

*Below right: The famous café after the war,*
*before its demolition*

The smoke, arguments and laughter continued on until well past midnight. In the morning, late night revellers would return to the café for a quiet breakfast and a cup of coffee before going to work. The mood would be very different from the night before. Writer and Berlin contemporary Matheo Quinz described the change: "In the early morning hours from eight to ten there is an infernal atmosphere: cold smoke, rancid powder, floor polish and dust."

Regulars at the Romanisches Café were careful not to incur the wrath of Herr Fiering, the landlord. Those who misbehaved were handed a note, which read "You are requested to leave our establishment upon payment of your drink, and never again to set foot here. Failure to comply with this request will render the offender liable to prosecution for breach of the peace." Expulsion was, for some, a cultural death sentence. One recipient of Fiering's missive chose to commit suicide rather than face a life without the Romanisches.

The famous west end café continued as a cultural Mecca after World War I. Thrown into this mix of painters, philosophers and dancers were the new personalities of the silver screen, director Billy Wilder among them. From his privileged vantage point in the swimmers' pool he could discuss his latest project with the likes of fellow director Robert Siodmak, oblivious to the aspiring actresses who tried to catch his attention a world away at the non-swimmers' tables.

By the early 1930s, leather-jacketed Gestapo men appeared on the scene, signalling the beginning of the end for the Romanisches. They and other Nazis with intellectual pretensions drove out the remaining elements of the artistic community, many of whom gravitated to Café Zuntz farther east on the Tauentzienstrasse.

After the war, what was once a lively area of movie theatres, shops and restaurants around the Romanisches Café was left a bleak landscape of half-ruined buildings. As the rubble was slowly being cleared away, exiled German architects such as Ludwig Mies van der Rohe and Martin Wagner returned to their country of birth to preach the virtues of "democratic" international modernism. In their view, traditional German designs of stone and brick that characterised buildings like the Romanisches evoked memories of a shameful past. The post-war skyline, they said, should be populated with bold monoliths of steel and glass.

In 1962, excavation work began on the south side of the Breitscheid Platz where the old café once stood. The new development to emerge over the next three years included an office tower and a 15,000 square metre shopping complex that reflected Germany's embrace of the international modernist movement. Just as the Europa Center's 22-storey American-style skyscraper stood in stark contrast to the ruined spire of the Kaiser Wilhelm Memorial Church, its revolving Mercedes-Benz star became an enduring symbol of West Berlin's post-war recovery.

*The Europa Center, post-war Berlin's glass and steel break*
*from the past*

# HAUS VATERLAND

The "House of the Fatherland" started out in 1912 as Haus Potsdam, yet another creation of Franz Schwechten, the prolific architect whose designs included the Romanisches Café, the Kaiser Wilhelm Memorial Church and the remarkable entrance gate to the AEG factory on the Brunnenstrasse. Situated next to the Potsdam Railway Station, this long, narrow building contained offices, restaurants, a cinema and a luxurious two-storey café called the Piccadilly. Haus Potsdam's name was changed to a more patriotic Haus Vaterland in 1914, the same year Café Piccadilly shed its British moniker to become the "Deutsches Caféhaus".

In 1927, entrepreneur Carl Stahl-Urach began a process that ultimately turned the former Café Piccadilly into a gastronomic fantasyland, the likes of which Berliners had never seen before. The complex, which was purchased and elaborated upon by restauranteur Hans Kempinski the following year, included a Viennese wine bar, a Spanish bodega and a Wild West saloon done up to look like a prairie cabin. The saloon was particularly colourful, featuring musicians dressed up in sombreros and chaparajos. They would play old favourites like the "Mexican Hat Dance" while a stuffed bear looked on.

Patrons were treated to the ultimate in 20's kitsch when they walked into Haus Vaterland's Löwenbräu beerhall. Every hour on the hour the stage lights dimmed, Fritz Färber's Bavarian ensemble put down their instruments and the sounds of distant thunder filled the hall. The rumbling grew louder and storm clouds descended, followed by artificial rain and lightning flashes. The rain turned into snow and the scene became one of winter. Then the clouds rolled back and the sun reappeared over a tranquil Alpine scene, signalling the band to take a final swig from their beer mugs and crank out another raucous set of polkas.

By 1942, the war economy and the restrictions it imposed on everyday life had led to general decline in good humour among Berliners.

*Opposite left: Haus Vaterland's famous Rheinterrasse
and its programme for the month of August, 1939.
Patrons could have a meal while being entertained by a
floorshow of singers, jugglers, and Rudi Paetzold's nine-piece
orchestra*

*Below: Haus Vaterland at night looking down the Stresemann-
strasse, circa 1935*

In response, Joseph Goebbels announced that the month of May would be a special "month of politeness", where Haus Vaterland employees, from ticket takers to bartenders, were among those urged to be less abrupt to their customers. The iniative featured a contest with prizes given away to 40 of the most polite individuals in his or her occupation.

By March 1945, all thoughts of manners had been replaced with ones of sheer survival. The Russians were closing in on the city limits, choking off supply routes that fed the city. Black market prices for the most basic food items skyrocketed. In an effort to avoid general starvation, the city government set up emergency food stations, one of which was located at Haus Vaterland. Where Berliners used to flock to Haus Vaterland for a pleasant night of diversion, they now descended in droves in search of any scrap of food that would prolong their lives.

During the years of Allied occupation, the boundary that divided the Russian and American sectors ran across the Potsdamer Platz directly in front of the entrance to the ruined Haus Vaterland. Most of the charred structure itself was a write-off, but a small restaurant bravely remained open for business for a short time. Like its ill-fated neighbour the Columbus Haus across the Potsdamer Platz, the partially-rebuilt Haus Vaterland went up in flames during the workers' uprising of June 17th, 1953.

Any lingering commercial value the building may have retained vanished eight years later with the construction of the Berlin Wall. In what used to be the hub of a thriving city, the ruins of Haus Vaterland now stood on a forgotten fringe of a divided city, its entrance blocked off by a 3-metre high concrete wall. In February of 1976, Franz Schwechten's crumbling relic was finally condemned as a public danger and pulled down. The story would have ended there had it not been for events of October and November 1989 when the Communist regime in East Germany collapsed in on itself, causing the sudden and quite unforeseen

*Right: Emergency food distribution at Haus Vaterland, March 1945*

*Below: View of Hans Kempinski's ruined entertainment complex during the first months of Allied occupation*

reunification of Berlin. The Wall was soon demolished, permitting traffic to once again circulate in front of the Haus Vaterland site on the Stresemannstrasse. A consortium of investors led by A + T subsequently acquired the Haus Vaterland site and began excavation work in 1996.

Compared with the more flamboyant DaimlerChrysler and Sony complexes nearby, the project, known as "Park Kolonnaden Potsdamer Platz", is more understated in terms of its height and external appearance. The north end of the complex is 12 storeys of rounded glass, evoking a blander, more modern version of Haus Vaterland's circular front tower. This portion of the complex is intended to serve as a hotel and conference centre. The total cost of the "Park Kolonnaden" is expected to top 500 million DM.

*Architect's model of the successor to Haus Vaterland, the "Park Kolonnaden Potsdamer Platz"*

*Opposite above: Haus Vaterland in 1966. The wall passes directly in front of the entrance at Stresemannstrasse*

*Below: View of the Stresemannstrasse in 2001, with the "Park Kolonnaden" (right)*

# LUTTER & WEGNER

*Above: Lutter & Wegner's historic wine cellar, where for years E.T.A. Hoffmann and his friend Ludwig Devrient met to consume prodigious quantities of champagne*

*Opposite: The famous wine house of Lutter & Wegner shown at its location on the Charlottenstrasse in 1936*

The wine house of Lutter & Wegner was, for many years, a haunt of artists both famous and obscure. Conveniently situated around the corner from the Royal Playhouse, the establishment dated back to 1811, when Berlin was a medium-sized town of 200,000 souls still living in the shadow of Napoleon's empire.

One of the first regulars who sampled Lutter & Wegner's selection of fine wines was actor and playwright August Wilhelm Iffland, who had been directing the Royal Playhouse on the Gendarmenmarkt since his recruitment from Mannheim in 1796. Iffland was an extremely talented individual, who introduced many new plays and concepts to Berlin's theatrical scene. Despite his broadminded approach to stagecraft, he also attempted to fulfil the secret desire of many a theatre director: in 1803, he tried to ban theatre reviews from appearing in city newspapers.

Another habitué of Lutter & Wegner was the leading light of Berlin's cultural community, E.T.A. Hoffmann. When he was not drawing inspiration from the many bottles of champagne in the establishment's wine cellar, he was either at home penning his latest manuscript or presiding as judge at the Prussian Kammergericht. Considered the greatest writer of his age, Hoffmann is best remembered for such macabre tales as the Dancing Doll, which portrayed the mad Kapellmeister Kreisler in vivid detail.

Hoffmann's drinking companion was Ludwig Devrient, regarded by many as 19th century Germany's most talented stage performer. The two would down prodigious amounts of sparkling wine in Lutter & Wegner's cellar and then spend equal amounts of energy avoiding the bill. Devrient's theatrics in the wine house were legendary. Already quite drunk, the actor would arrive at the café, then stumble down the lower staircase bellowing "Gib mir ein Glas Sekt, Schurke!" (Give me a cup of sack, rogue!) — a quote from Shakespeare's Henry IV. The waiters knew

Devrient meant champagne, not sherry, and his corruption of the word stuck. To this day, sparkling wine in Germany is referred to as Sekt.

Hoffmann and Devrient's antics gained a certain amount of notoriety at the wine house over the years and the management attracted a good deal of extra customers as a result. The proprietor, J.C. Lutter, once tore up the two men's tab rather than see his famous guests carry out their threat to move to Schonert's across the street. He again tore up Hoffmann's tab following the writer's premature death at the age of 46.

Long after Devrient himself passed away, portraits of the two famous regulars hung in the front room of the tavern. Next to the portrait was one of Devrient's favourite quotes, "Indifference to champagne is hypocrisy; don't be cold when it comes on ice."

The 18th century building that housed Lutter & Wegner was designed by master builder Karl von Gontard, the same individual who was responsible for the twin churches on the Gendarmenmarkt and many fine residences on the Unter den Linden. An upper storey to Gontard's building was added in 1937, only to be eliminated by Allied bombs six years later.

A truncated version of Lutter & Wegner's wine shop continued to operate out of the building's basement after the war, but business in the eastern part of Berlin did not flourish. Eventually the remains of Lutter & Wegner were demolished and replaced with a parking lot. The historical

*Above: The establishment did not thrive during the GDR years, as this 1956 photo of Lutter & Wegner attests*

*Right: The bombed-out remains of Lutter & Wegner after the war*

Weinstube had in the meantime moved across town to the Schlüter-strasse in Charlottenburg, where it remains to this day.

Throughout the GDR years, the site of the demolished Lutter & Wegner languished in a particularly drab part of the Mitte district. Its neighbouring streets were quiet and lifeless. Traffic was sparse; few shops and even fewer restaurants could be found. At times, patrolling soldiers of the National People's Army (NVA) seemed to outnumber the civilian population.

While the area still lacks the bustle of pre-war Berlin, the area around Hoffmann's favourite hangout has experienced a much-needed transformation. A spate of luxury hotels, several fine restaurants and Berlin's first gentleman's club — The Havana Lounge — have sprung up around the Gendarmenmarkt recently, making this part of Berlin a magnet for the upwardly-mobile.

The East German parking lot where Lutter & Wegner once stood is now occupied by the posh Four Season's Hotel. Directly above the cellar where Hoffmann and Devrient once raised their glasses, a richly appointed foyer of sparkling marble now greets a rarefied class of well-heeled travellers.

On April 30th, 1997, another Lutter & Wegner wine house opened up just a block south of its original location on the Charlottenstrasse. Its kitchens quickly attracted praise from high places. A visiting gastronome from the New York Times vowed that "in all of Vienna you won't find a better Wiener Schnitzel than at Lutter & Wegner".

*49 Charlottenstrasse is now home to the Four Season's Hotel. Its understated exterior is deceptive: guests of the house are treated to some of the most opulent bathrooms in Berlin*

# KAISERHOF

Around the time of modern Germany's founding, an entrepreneur called Sebastian Hensel took one look at the city's hotels and called them, "a mockery of the travelling world." He set out to remedy the situation by erecting a hotel whose rooms Emperor William II himself was to grumble were better appointed than his own chambers in the Imperial Palace.

Construction of the Kaiserhof started on the west side of the Wilhelmplatz in 1873. When it officially opened on October 1st, 1875, it was without a doubt the most opulent hotel in Berlin and would remain so until the Hotel Adlon opened on the Pariser Platz 30 years later.

The Kaiserhof was the epitome of Wilhelmine modernity, outfitted with a steam-generated heating plant, electric light, private baths, pneumatic elevators and a new invention called the telephone. In the kitchen, a staff of French chefs and sous-chefs had been lured from Paris to labour over the Kaiserhof's modern gas stoves.

The quality of the food and the opulence of its ballrooms persuaded Otto von Bismarck to welcome the heads of Europe's great powers here during the Berlin Conference of 1878.

Unfortunately for Hensel, his new hotel was in business for just nine days before a calamitous fire struck. The blaze was so fierce that it took two days to extinguish. Despite this early setback, the hotel was rebuilt and quickly went on to earn its investors a handsome dividend. Berlin was in the middle of the "Gründerzeit", a period of great expansion that followed the founding of the Second Reich, and there was no shortage of affluent guests in need of comfortable lodgings. Some stayed to conduct business in the burgeoning financial district nearby, while others were merely passing through on their way north to the posh new seaside resorts on the Baltic coast.

Past guests of the Kaiserhof were not restricted to financiers and wealthy holidaymakers, they also included leading men of science, such

*Right: Turn-of-the-century brochure of the Kaiserhof when it was still part of the Atlantic hotel chain, a firm that also ran the Palast on the Potsdamer Platz*

*Below: View of the Kaiserhof from across the Wilhelmplatz in the late 1930s*

as the renowned physician Robert Koch, and the first winner of the Nobel Prize for Physics, Wilhelm Konrad von Röntgen. Other guests who signed the registry book were Manuel II, King of Portugal and his companion, a young revue starlet called Gaby Deslys. (Their ongoing affair nearly cost the king his throne.) The emperor's 61-year-old sister Viktoria and her 27-year-old consort, former Kaiserhof dishwasher Alexander Zubkow, would later spend the occasional night of romance here.

The fall of the 500-year old Hohenzollern dynasty in 1918 meant that the Kaiserhof's ballrooms would no longer hold glittering receptions for the Imperial General Staff. In fact, its royalist name may have become something of a liability during the years of the Weimar Republic, but by the end of the decade the Kaiserhof had become a hotel for the powerful once again.

In April of 1930, a relative unknown called Adolf Hitler and his colleague Joseph Goebbels appeared at the front desk and rented one of the cheapest rooms in the house. Three years later, they would occupy the entire top floor of the 262-room hotel, using Suites 140 to 142 as their headquarters while they consolidated their influence in the Reichstag.

Hitler did not always sleep peacefully in his bed, however. At one point he became convinced that the hotel's kitchen staff had been infiltrated by communists and suspected they were plotting to poison his food. Goebbels' wife, Magda, put his fears to rest by preparing meals from her nearby home and sending them over in specially insulated containers. Sometimes Hitler and his press attaché Ernst Hanfstaengl

*A group of American servicemen tour the city's ruins in 1946. Here they visit the gutted Kaiserhof and the neighbouring Reich Chancellery*

would take a break from their plotting and take the elevator down to the hotel's palm court for a little diversion. They would take a seat at their favourite table in a corner next to some potted plants and listen to the hotel's pseudo-Hungarian orchestra. Often, word would get around that the future Chancellor was there and swarms of overdressed women wearing furs and too much perfume would file in and hover in their vicinity.

As with all the other hotels in Berlin, the war years were extremely bad for business. The Kaiserhof's steadily declining guest list reached ground zero on November 23rd, 1943, when an air raid levelled the hotel and much of central Berlin besides. The only part that survived was the Kaiserhof's luxurious bunker, which remained well stocked with brandy and cigars until the last hours of the "Third Reich".

After the war, the remains of the Kaiserhof were razed. By 1975, it had been replaced with an architectural eyesore that continues to house the "Office for the Protection of the Interests of the Korean People's Democratic Republic". Although the Kaiserhof was long gone, its foundations remained a concern of the Ministry for State Security (Stasi) during the GDR years. The Stasi obtained the building plans of the old hotel to make sure none of its long-dormant cellars and air raid bunkers could be used as a potential escape route to the west.

*Above: A child plays in the sand in front of the Kaiserhof entrance, 1947*

*Right: The North Korean legation continues to operate from their dated building on the Kaiserhof site, as they have done since 1975*

# ADLON HOTEL

After Napoleon's armies swept into Berlin on their way to Moscow, the little emperor demanded that members of the government of Frederick William III sign an oath of loyalty to France. Most public servants meekly complied, but one of the few to resist this humiliation was Count Wilhelm Friedrich von Redern. This same individual commissioned the young architect Karl Friedrich Schinkel two decades later to design his residence on the Pariser Platz. The Neo-Florentine design of Schinkel attracted the attention of many admirers, from Goethe to the king himself.

The Redern Palace stood on the south-east corner of the Pariser Platz for the remainder of the 19th century, gradually accumulating a patina of grit from the city's rising levels of air pollution. The palace's sooty presence in full view of the Brandenburg Gate became a source of great embarrassment to Emperor William II. As someone who preferred highly ornamented buildings with expressive displays of historical romanticism, he also detested the simplicity of Redern's Neo-Classical residence, referring to it as "an old barn". He yearned to be rid of it.

As luck would have it, restauranteur Lorenz Adlon also wanted to demolish the Redern Palace, but for different reasons. He had plans to

*Far left: The "Grand Salon", circa 1907. The banquet table's fine linens came from Grunfeld's on the Leipziger Strasse*

*Left: The Adlon's "Grand Salon" after the mysterious fire that destroyed the old hotel in May, 1945*

*Right: Count Redern's Neo-Florentine palace on the Pariser Platz.
Built in 1829-31, it included a ballroom of white marble and
a picture gallery filled with paintings of the old school by
Poussin, Lairesse, Tintoretto and Bellini. Count Arnim's palace
can be seen in the background to the right*

*Below: Lorenz Adlon's sumptuous new hotel, which opened
in 1907, the same year the neighbouring Arnim Palace became
home to the Prussian Academy of Art*

*Left: The Adlon's bricked-up entrance on May 4th, 1945. White flags of surrender still fly from the upper balcony*

build a sparkling new hotel that would be the envy of all of Europe. The emperor, after hearing of Adlon's venture, gave the project his whole-hearted support, even going so far as to personally help with the financing.

Thanks in part to the emperor's gold, Lorenz Adlon was able to spare no expense in the construction of his grand new hotel. It cost 20 million marks to build, just a few million marks less than the state paid to build the Reichstag. Part of the money went to purchase great quantities of yellow carrara marble that had to be shipped in by truck from Italy. The rest went to pay for such refinements as hand-wrought staircase railings and sumptuous rugs from Gerson's.

On October 23rd, 1907, the Hotel Adlon opened its doors. An army of pages in their light blue uniforms were on hand to serve what would become a legendary procession of world-famous guests, including Enrico Caruso, Tsar Nicholas II of Russia, Henry Ford and Charlie Chaplin. Lorenz Adlon and his son Louis were never far away, fussing over their customers as if they were old and respected friends.

Despite its aura of respectability, the hotel had its share of intrigue between the two world wars. One of the most famous criminal cases of the twenties took place in its plush suites. In the summer of 1924, a 50-year-old mailman called Lange disappeared on his way to the Adlon with a special delivery for Baron Winterfeld. Lange was later found in a room neighbouring Winterfeld's, bound to a chair and strangled with a curtain cord. His mailbag, containing 41 letters with 240,000 marks inside, was empty.

Three years later, the culprit was finally brought to justice. As it turned out, he had just written a play about the murder of a postman in the Adlon. "All I hope is that it will be put on before my execution," said the accused from his cell. "If it is a success, I shall feel that I have not lived in vain."

*The Adlon in 1946. To the left is a placard of Josef Stalin,*
*the "Supreme Generalissimo" of Soviet Russia*

Throughout the war, Lorenz Adlon's son remained at his post, trying with diminishing success to maintain the hotel's famous pre-war standards. When the first air raids struck the city, he had a huge wire net erected over the hotel roof. For the first two years, the bombs would strike the net and harmlessly bounce off, but after 1943 the bombs grew larger and more lethal. Fortunately, the hotel was spared any direct hits and continued to operate effectively throughout the entire duration of the war.

Even with the advancing Red Army just kilometres away, the hotel did its best to keep up appearances. SS commander Leon Degrelle, who was in the Adlon celebrating Hitler's last birthday, described how the establishment "was still operating in spite of the bombs and the shells falling right into the streets. In the brilliantly lit restaurant, tuxedoed waiters and maîtres d'hôtel in tails continued solemnly and impressively to serve purple slices of kohlrabi on huge silver platters."

The Adlon actually survived the war relatively intact, but on May 3rd, 1945, a disastrous fire raged though its floors, the day Russian troops arrived and cleaned out its famous wine cellars. The leaping flames were filmed by a Russian news crew.

The only part of the hotel to survive the fire was the so-called Courier's Wing. Initially, the only working entrance was through a gap in the ruins on the Wilhelmstrasse. The visitor had to ascend a narrow flight of service stairs then walk down a red-carpeted corridor to a small room packed with tables. The dining area was poorly furnished except for two paintings by the Brueghel brothers. Food could only be ordered by those holding the appropriate ration coupons; 200 potato points, 5 fat points and 100 meat points could, in 1945, get you a plate of meat-loaf. In the back of the restaurant, fifteen rooms were still habitable. Occupied almost continually by Russian officers, they were periodically raided by military MPs in search of unauthorised female visitors.

In the years that followed, the Adlon's 15 surviving rooms were expanded to 70, still a fraction of its original 325. Like other private concerns in the East, the Adlon was eventually expropriated by the state and handed over to the state-run consumer outlet. The décor was altered to suit the new age of socialism — the rebuilt foyer and halls were now festooned with patriotic slogans and stern-faced portraits of Wilhelm Pieck, Otto Grotewohl and other SED party luminaries.

In its final incarnation, this drab fragment of the Adlon served as the home to the Ministry of Education. The building was finally pulled down in 1984.

Early in 1995, a horde of 1,200 construction workers from six countries descended on the vacant site next to the Brandenburg Gate to begin construction of a new, resurrected Adlon. Their efforts were soon rewarded: dredging operations unearthed a few hardy survivors of Louis Adlon's legendary wine collection — six intact bottles of 1941 red burgundy.

*Opposite: A tradition of high living returns; on April 4th, 1997, the Adlon reopened with great ceremony. By April of the following year, its guests had already consumed 67,320 bottles of champagne*

The completed hotel opened in June of 1997. Its exterior bears a reasonable likeness to the beloved pre-war establishment, although the interior has been completely redesigned. Guests who enter the lobby are greeted by one of the few original remnants of the old hotel: a sparkling fountain that once stood in the Adlon garden. As they traverse an expanse of marble and slate floors, they can rest in an arrangement of Empire style armchairs and sofas.

The new proprietors of the Adlon have managed to retain the ambience of hushed refinement that was the trademark of its predecessor, though in some ways they have become a victim of their own success. Efforts must continually be made to repel the crowds of admiring tourists who are tempted to dart inside for a quick peek at the world of luxury within.

# THE EXCELSIOR

Today, a featureless high-rise stands on the Stresemannstrasse directly across from a ruined fragment of the former Anhalt railway station. Fifty years ago, when trains still pulled into the station and the street went by another name, this address was occupied by the largest hotel in Europe, the Excelsior. Connected to the railway terminus by underground tunnel, this gigantic establishment was touted as "a town in itself", complete with a row of retail shops, a dance hall, an in-house tailor and shoemaker, a 7,000 volume library, and nine different restaurants. The hotel even published its own newspaper, which appeared daily except on public holidays.

Everything about the 600-room hotel was monumental in size. In the basement a vast beer cellar lined with white tiles could seat 1,500 diners. Upstairs, a grandiose ballroom with full-size palm trees and topped with an enormous stained-glass skylight could accommodate hundreds of dancers at a time. Just off the main entrance was the Hotel Café where, beneath electric chandeliers and wall sconces, guests could choose from no less than 200 newspapers and periodicals from around the world.

A brochure from the 1930s boasted not only of the hotel's size, but also of its state of the art equipment. "This wonderful and gigantic building is the supreme triumph of modern hotel technics. The Excelsior is 'the' hotel on the Continent without coal: heating and hot water are provided by the very latest high-pressure gas plant." Other technological marvels included a telephone and radio in almost every room.

Management made every attempt to keep its guests refreshed, fed and entertained. The hotel's owner, Kurt Elschner, would say, "In my house you can eat without fuss, sleep, drink, read, work, hold conferences, shop, bank money, dance and enjoy yourself. In a word, you can be happy without having to go out." He neglected to mention the in-house

*Above left: The Excelsior's American Bar, which had a loyal following among Berlin's international press corps*
*Above right: Pre-war hotel brochure, which described the Excelsior as the largest hotel on the European continent*

*Opposite: The Hotel Excelsior on 78 Stresemannstrasse, circa 1935*

male and female prostitutes who were also on hand to tend to the guests' more intimate needs.

The hotel's sheer size was to inspire more than its paying guests. Author Vicki Baum worked for several days in the hotel to soak up its atmosphere, prior to writing "Menschen im Hotel". Her novel was later made into a film, the classic "Grand Hotel" starring Greta Garbo and Joan Crawford.

A staunch monarchist who was once named "Geheimer Kommerzien-rat" at the behest of the emperor's wife, Herr Elschner regarded the rising Nazi influence in Berlin with distaste. At first, he refused to let any of Hitler's followers set foot in his establishment, prompting the party to blacklist his business in 1933. Eventually, he caved in to their attempts to ruin him and permitted the destruction of a few panels of stained glass with Jewish motifs.

The grand façade of the Excelsior collapsed onto the street during the last days of World War II, a victim of artillery shells, bombs and street fighting. The ruins of the hotel continued to loom over the newly renamed Saarlandstrasse for the better part of a decade, but by 1954 no trace of the Excelsior remained.

The 1960s-era Excelsior Haus that today occupies the site of the old hotel bears no resemblance to its predecessor. This 18-storey eyesore is a good example of post-war building practices in Berlin that tended to maximise commercial and residential space at the expense of aesthetic considerations.

*Above left: One of the hotel's spacious kitchens. In 1939, a cook at the Excelsior was paid 260 Reichmarks a month*

*Above right: Italian foreign minister Count Galeazzo Ciano inspects an honour guard at the Anhalt railway station. The Excelsior Hotel can be seen in the background*

*Above right: The Excelsior in the summer of 1952, shortly before its demolition. To the right is the north entrance to the abandoned Anhalt station*

*Below right: The old hotel was replaced by the Excelsior Haus, a modernist skyscraper built in the 1960s. It was meant to bring life back to the devastated neighbourhood*

# THE ESPLANADE

Few of us today would guess that the former repertory theatre now encapsulated within the Sony Centre was once an elegant hotel situated in a tranquil neighbourhood of art galleries and townhouses. By Berlin standards, the Esplanade was a comfortable establishment when it first opened in 1908, with over 400 rooms, 102 baths, and a luxurious restaurant operated by the Ritz Carlton group. Its opulence was enhanced during a 1911-12 expansion phase that added a palm court and a 1600-square-metre dining room accented with Pavonazza marble. At 10 to 15 marks a night, the Esplanade was the second most expensive hotel in Berlin after the Adlon.

The Esplanade's understated luxury quickly earned it the reputation of the hotel of choice for Brandenburg's landed gentry during their occasional trips into town. Even though the Adlon was a degree more extravagant, it was also frequented by movie stars, politicians, industrialists and other arrivistes, the sort of people good Junkers tried to avoid.

The establishment's quiet gentility was interrupted on May 1st, 1916, when a mob of protesters stormed the Esplanade kitchens and stole all its bread. The resulting mess was soon cleaned up, but the disruption was a harbinger of the social turmoil to come. By then, the war was going badly for the Kaiser and much of Berlin was starving. In her diaries that same year, Princess von Blücher recalled the dirty looks she got at the Esplanade when a downtrodden passer-by glared at her through the hotel's glass door.

In the years following the Armistice of 1918, the sight of an aristocrat and his wife sipping tea in the palm court became increasingly rare. As Berlin's economy deteriorated, a less pedigreed type of hotel guest began to wander the hotel's gracious hallways — the lower-middle class foreigner with hard currency to spend. Until fiscal stability returned in

*Left: The Esplanade's interior court garden in 1908*

*Below: The opulent Palm Court, one of the few salons to survive the destruction of World War II*

*Below: The Esplanade on Bellevuestrasse shortly after it opened in 1908. Prussia's nobility preferred the rooms here to those of the arriviste Adlon*

1924, rivers of champagne priced in rapidly devaluing marks could be ordered by any guest with a few dollars in his pocket. While a clerk from Chicago could live it up in his rented three-room suite, the hotel's manager was left to drag home sacks of bank notes worth less per pound than cattle bones.

The Esplanade managed to avoid serious damage from Allied bombs throughout most of the war but on February 5th, 1945, the hotel suffered seven direct hits, destroying its two uppermost floors. Its shattered kitchens reopened 23 days later, only to be bombed out a second time. This time, damage was not quite as severe, and the hotel staff managed to serve up fried potatoes to their shell-shocked guests the next day. Despite this resourcefulness, the Esplanade would not survive as a hotel for much longer. Three-quarters destroyed, only a marble staircase, a few salons and a few 1908-vintage bathrooms was all that remained by the end of the war.

As one of the only buildings in the area around the Potsdamer Platz even remotely serviceable after the war, a chopped-down version of the old hotel underwent some emergency repairs and briefly reopened in 1949. Thereafter, it continued to eke out a marginal existence at the edge of the British sector, first as a dance hall, then as a discount movie theatre.

Reunification has rescued the Esplanade from its years of seedy isolation next to the Wall. Its status as a protected landmark prompted its new owners, the Sony Corporation and its partners Tishman Speyer and Kajima, to come up with an imaginative way to integrate the architectural detail of the former hotel within the surrounding 1.5 billion-DM Sony Complex.

Efforts at saving fragments of the Esplanade have been as painstaking as they have been innovative. While little effort was required to

restore the old hotel's sandstone façade to its Wilhelmine splendour, the salons inside posed a larger problem. In its existing configuration, the sidewalk of the proposed new Potsdamer Strasse behind the complex would have sliced through the back of the Emperor's Salon (Kaisersaal), a splendid Neo-Baroque ballroom the emperor once used to hold his famous stag parties. After some negotiation with the Senate, the Sony consortium agreed to relocate it. For structural reasons, however, the entire Emperor's Salon had to be moved as a single unit. To accomplish this Herculean task, the 1,300-ton salon was reinforced with concrete supports and steel girders, then gently raised up by a crane at a rate of 1 cm per minute, twisted 90 degrees, and placed on air-cushioned supports. It was then sent down a steel track on a computer-driven dolly and transported 75 meters away to its final resting spot next to the old Palm Court.

Meanwhile, the former Breakfast Salon was broken up into 500 pieces and reassembled nearby. Two of its walls were left behind, protected behind glass, to serve as a visual time capsule of the Esplanade in its damaged post-war state. The remaining portion of the translocated salon is now occupied by a Parisian-style café. Special events take place in these and other salons of the former Esplanade, providing a genteel counterpoint to the ultra-modern exhibition areas of the Sony Complex itself.

*Opposite: The granite remnants of the Esplanade just before its entombment in the façade of the Sony Centre*

*Below: View of the Esplanade with construction of the Sony Centre in full swing, spring 2001*

# KAUFHAUS DES WESTENS

The pre-war photo to the right looks from the Wittenbergplatz westward down the Tauentzienstrasse towards the hazy spires of the Kaiser Wilhelm Memorial Church. To the left stands the oldest surviving luxury department store in Berlin, the Kaufhaus des Westens (KaDeWe).

KaDeWe rose on the south-west corner of the Wittenbergplatz in 1906, at a time when this part of the city was starting to edge out the Leipziger Strasse as a fashionable place to shop. KaDeWe's owners, a consortium of three investors led by Adolf Jandorf, aimed to cash in on the growing market for luxury goods fed by the recent migration of Berlin's moneyed classes to the western suburbs of Charlottenburg and Wilmersdorf.

In sharp contrast to the stone and glass palace that Messel created for Wertheim on the Leipziger Platz, architect Johann Emil Schaudt chose a more understated theme for KaDeWe. While the structure's exterior window pattern was designed to blend in with the surrounding neighbourhood of Wilhelmine apartment blocks, its interior would be the epitome of sophisticated modernity, one that included, among other things, light fixtures designed by architect Peter Behrens.

In a bid to cater to his customers' every need, Jandorf installed a hairdresser's salon, dressmaker's shop, travel agency and food court among his 24,000 square metres of fine merchandise. The store was also equipped with the latest in building technology. A comprehensive system of 850 automatic alarms guarded KaDeWe's five floors against possible fire while an 18-kilometre long network of pneumatic tubes kept its hundreds of employees in constant touch with one another.

*KaDeWe during the Weimar years. In the foreground is the Wittenbergplatz subway station, designed by the prolific Alfred Grenander and completed in 1913*

During Berlin's sinful "Golden Twenties", other, less savoury transactions took place just beyond KaDeWe's heavy bronze doors. A young, unemployed migrant called Carl Zuckmayer began a mercifully brief career in front of Jandorf's emporium as a sidewalk hustler. His pockets filled with cigars, cigarettes, and little envelopes filled with "koks" (cocaine), the young man stood in front of KaDeWe hissing the words, "Tsssigars, Tssigarettes?" at passers-by. If a prospect responded with a snuffle, he was instructed to produce one of his little white packets. He narrowly escaped arrest after a Polish prostitute alerted him to an undercover policeman who had been watching his antics from across the street.

Shortly after Zuckmayer had moved on to become one of Weimar Germany's most celebrated playwrights, Jandorf's consortium sold KaDeWe to its arch rival Hermann Tietz. Beginning in 1926, KaDeWe hosted Tietz's famous February "White Sales" (Weisse Woche), an event that nightly lit up Schaudt's building with brilliant neon lettering.

KaDeWe's tradition of providing feather pillows and silk shirts to Berlin's upper class was brutally interrupted on Tuesday November 23rd, 1943, when a warning of heavy air raids (Luftgefahr 15) was broadcast over the city. A heavy rain had been falling all day, and as a result of the poor visibility in the skies above, crowds of people who gathered in the streets of Berlin's West End expected little damage. But it turned out to be one of the most effective bombing sorties of the war. During this attack, the Kaiser Wilhelm Memorial Church lost its main spire and the KaDeWe department store went up in flames.

After the war, the owners of KaDeWe decided to rebuild. They contracted architect Hans Soll to redesign the structure's ruined roof and simplify its exterior façade. In the summer of 1950, after an initial reconstruction phase had restored its lower two floors, KaDeWe was ready for business. At 11 a.m. on its opening day, the store's porter unlocked the front doors

*White sales at Kaufhaus des Westens in the 1920s...with pyjamas on sale for 9 marks*

*Opposite above: A night shot of KaDeWe in the twenties
shows Berliners' infatuation with neon lighting*

*Below: The fire-gutted department store after the war.
The building from which the photo on the previous page was
taken, has been reduced to a pile of bricks (far left)*

and instantly found himself overwhelmed by crowds of eager shoppers. Within minutes the frazzled employee was forced to close the doors again as the local police tried to deal with all the pushing and shoving. Shoppers who survived the initial mêlée were eventually rewarded with a bounty of scarce items like Philco television sets, General Electric radios, fur coats and French cosmetics.

Successive post-war renovations progressively enlarged KaDeWe's floorspace. In 1956, the department store's now-famous food hall was opened on the sixth floor; another 120 million DM renovation completed in 1978 boosted the retail space to 44,000 square metres.

KaDeWe's regular expansion mirrored West Berlin's ability to prosper in an isolated enclave deep in communist territory. Berliners showed they could let bygones be bygones when they dropped coins and banknotes through the hole drilled in the roof of a Trabant automobile inside KaDeWe's main hall in Christmas of 1990. The proceeds were part of the "Convoy for Siberia" campaign that was intended to aid hungry Russians following the recent collapse of the Soviet regime.

Yet another renovation project that began in 1991 and ended in 1996 added a rooftop restaurant, a new glazed arch over the main entrance and 16,000 more square metres of floor space to the historic department store. Its grand opening on September 25th, 1996, attracted an impressive 200,000 visitors. Today, KaDeWe is the largest retail outlet on the European continent.

*The bottom two floors of KaDeWe reopened to the public in 1950. By 1956, the remaining four floors had been restored. This photo shows the store's latest addition, a glazed rooftop archway over its main entrance*

# TIETZ

At the turn of the last century an energetic retailer called Hermann Tietz arrived in Berlin, confident that there were profits to be made in the capital's booming retail trade. His timing was impeccable. Berlin's expanding links by rail and sea to diverse suppliers around the globe meant that Tietz could offer his customers products they had never seen before. Meanwhile, mass-production techniques in factories within Germany let him buy in bulk, filling his aisles with mountains of pots, pans and other hardware at prices a traditional shopkeeper could never match. The recent flood of mass-circulation newspapers that started to appear on every street corner also meant he could advertise his wares across the city cheaply and effectively.

Many nonetheless questioned Tietz's decision in 1904 to open a new store on the Alexanderplatz, in a neighbourhood that had seen better days. In reply to these nay-sayers, Tietz would give a little chuckle and reply, "I don't need good locations. I make them!" Tietz's new store was impressive. Oversized statuary loomed over the front doors, greeting shoppers like stony guardians of Ali Baba's treasure-filled cave. At night his trademark, a four-metre wide glass and steel globe, was lit up high overhead, a glowing beacon that pointed to the fabulous delights that lay inside.

Tietz's aim was to turn shopping from a chore into an adventure. Besides providing rarities like rice and oranges, he was the first retailer to introduce the tomato to suspicious Berliners. After Hermann Tietz's death in 1907, his son Georg carried on the family tradition and in 1925 added to the shopping experience by installing Berlin's first escalator in the Leipziger Strasse store.

Georg also used his marketing savvy to introduce the concept of "White Weeks" (Weisse Wochen) during the traditionally quiet month of February. For one month, the entire store would become a dazzling

*Opposite far left: A 1909 photo of Tietz' sumptuous carpet showroom*

*Opposite left: The department store's light-filled central court in 1910*

*Below: Hermann Tietz's mammoth shopping emporium which stood for 40 years on the north side of the Alexanderplatz*

"melody of white", with its central atrium done up in elaborate displays that on any one day could be an Indian temple, a sailing ship or Roman Arch draped with white dry goods of every description. The "White Weeks" concept was so successful, it was quickly adopted by Tietz's competitors.

By 1933, the Tietz family managed the largest privately-owned chain of department stores in Europe. Unfortunately, their success attracted jealousy and resentment from Germany's new rulers. Nazi philosophy was hostile to the nation's large, cosmopolitan, and often Jewish-owned retail giants. They were seen as pandering to the public's sense of materialism while taking business away from local "German" shops.

Inevitably, the Tietz family had their business confiscated as part of Hitler's "Aryanisation" programme. The business was renamed "Hertie", an abbreviated version of its founder's full name.

After losing their business, the Tietz family was forced to flee Germany and eventually ended up in the United States in 1941. Meanwhile, the range of goods offered at their Alexanderplatz outlet grew less and less enticing. The war machine swallowed up an enormous slice of the nation's wealth, leaving very little for the average Berliner to consume. After a while, it seemed that everything was ersatz. Stores like Tietz were forced to sell men's suits made out of cellulose — a material derived from wood. The common joke went, "if you get holes in your suit, take off its shoots and use them as elbow patches."

After the war, the badly-damaged Tietz department store lay in ruins, its trademark globe drooped pathetically over the front entrance like an oversized steel orchid. By then, commerce had migrated from Tietz's fire-blackened interior to the open spaces of the Alexanderplatz.
There, Russian soldiers flush with three years' back pay carried out a brief but costly trade with the newly-arrived American troops. By taking

*Right: July, 1945: A female Russian MP directs traffic in front of the destroyed department store*

*Below: The Tietz ruins in 1945*

advantage of the Russian's mania for wristwatches, many American GIs made an instant fortune demanding — and getting — 10,000 reichmarks (well over $1,000 US) for their Mickey Mouse watches. The profits were handsome; the watches sold for just $7.50 at the US Army PX store.

By November 1945, Soviet MPs put a stop to all the action and quiet briefly returned to Tietz's ruins before the bulldozers finally levelled the place. In the late 1960s, the communist central planners authorized architect Josef Kaiser to design plans for construction of the Warenhaus Centrum (Centrum Department Store) on the site of Tietz's outlet, in a bid to rejuvenate the barren expanse that was once the hub of eastern Berlin. Kaiser is best known for his ill-fated Foreign Office complex that was built across from the Zeughaus (Armoury) on the site of Schinkel's Bauakademie (Academy of Architecture). Both buildings sported an exterior of coated white aluminium panels whose effect was intended to achieve a sense of "calm and monumentality". The state-owned department store opened its doors in 1970 and for the next twenty years offered East Berliners a range of shoddy products to which Herr Tietz would never have given shelf space. After unification, the Centrum Department Store was bought by the Kaufhof retailing giant. It renovated its new acquisition's interior but apart from the Kaufhof sign and its green trademark flags that flutter from its roof, the GDR-era structure remains outwardly unchanged.

*East German architect Josef Kaiser's vision of*
*"calm monumentality" on the Alexanderplatz.*
*"Aryanised", nationalised, then privatised:*
*the Tietz site is now controlled by the Kaufhof*
*retail chain*

# KARSTADT

Our modern day department store can trace its origins back to the late 19th century when merchants like Rudolph Karstadt saw the commercial benefits of amalgamating a variety of shops under one roof. Karstadt's first retail outlet, a manufacturing, confection, and fabrics emporium, opened in Wismar in 1881.

Instead of using barter to conduct his business as was the tradition at the time, Karstadt dealt strictly in cash and did his best to combine low prices with a high sales volume. His formula seemed to work and in 1920 he merged his expanding retail empire with Theodor Althoff's haberdashery, wool and linen stores under the name Rudolph Karstadt Corporation (Rudolph Karstadt AG).

To succeed in Berlin, Karstadt had to break into a retail market that was already thick with competitors. Hermann Tietz had been engaged in a decades-long battle with the Wertheim family on the Leipziger Strasse, while the consortium led by Adolf Jandorf vied for customers at his sumptuous Kaufhaus des Westens in the New West End. During a phase of rapid expansion in the Weimar years that saw its number of outlets swell to 89, Karstadt chose to set up shop in a part of Berlin that had been overlooked by the city's other department stores — the Neukölln district.

On June 21st, 1929, Karstadt opened a gleaming new retail outlet on the west side of the Hermannplatz. Designed by Hamburg architect Paul Schäfer, the new department store's sweeping vertical lines combined to create an illusion of height far greater than the building's actual size. "We have achieved the American dream," proclaimed an architectural handbook issued for the inaugural celebration.

The seven-storey structure provided 340,000 square metres of office and retail space, making it the largest department store in the city at the time. On the roof, in the shadows of its twin towers, a garden and

*Above: Two views taken 70 years apart of the Hermannplatz subway station. Designed by architect Alfred Grenander, the subway offered and offers direct access to Karstadt's basement*

*Opposite: Construction of the new Karstadt department store on the Hermannplatz in Neukölln. When complete, it became the largest retail outlet in Berlin*

restaurant offered customers a commanding 360-degree view of south-central Berlin.

The new Karstadt building was an impressive sight, even at night. Its two 15 metre-high rooftop columns shot a beam of light high into Berlin's evening skies, creating a landmark that pilots used over the next fifteen years to find their way to the nearby Tempelhof airport.

In addition to its eye-catching exterior, Karstadt's newest store had another advantage — it was connected by underground passage to Alfred Grenander's recently-completed Hermannplatz subway station. With the exception of Tietz on the Alexanderplatz, no other major department store offered this convenience.

During the war, Karstadt management had an increasingly difficult time keeping goods on their shelves. A strict rationing system and a gradual strangulation of supply lines to the city meant that more and more customers had to be turned away.

Ultimately, with the Russians just a few miles away and food supplies in the city almost completely depleted, the department store was set upon by looters. Half-starved Berliners swarmed down the aisles, grabbing noodles, marmalade, tins of condensed milk and anything else they could lay their hands on.

Later that afternoon, a squad of SS men arrived and laid charges around the building's foundations. They were acting on orders to deny the advancing Russians the 29 million mark's worth of supplies that still lay in the department store's basement. The Karstadt building was detonated on the 26th of April, the same day that the last telephone links connecting Berlin to the rest of Germany were cut. Soldiers of the advancing Red Army entered Karstadt's smoking ruins later that afternoon.

The political changes to sweep post-war Germany presented a setback to the Karstadt corporation. In 1945, the year after its 86-year-old founder

*Opposite far left: The splendid rooftop terrace and restaurant, seen from Karstadt's south-east tower looking north. Opposite left: Karstadt's distinctive architecture is used to good effect in a 1930s magazine advertisement*

*Above right: Karstadt in 1931, two years after its grand opening*

*Below right: Karstadt in ruins. Only a small fragment of the original structure survived the war*

died, Karstadt AG was left with just 45 of its 67 pre-war outlets. The other 22 stores lay either in the Soviet zone of Germany, or in the East Prussian territories that had been annexed by Poland and the USSR.

Fortunately for its owners, the Karstadt outlet on the Hermannplatz was situated in the American sector. In the 1950s, the retailer built a temporary four-storey structure on the south-west corner of the square and gradually expanded their premises in the years that followed.

Today, the department store remains very much in business. Except for a small portion of its western wing and a few vintage stair-cases, however, nothing remains of Schaefer's original 1920s design. For years Karstadt's post-war layout remained somewhat drab, but a recent makeover has sought to bring back some of the excitement that surrounded the launch of the original store here over 60 years ago.

*The refurbished Karstadt building,*
*based on plans by Jürgen Sawade*

# BEROLINA HAUS AND ALEXANDER HAUS

In the late 1920s, an Aschinger restaurant and a row of decrepit homes along the Königsgraben were demolished to make way for an ambitious new development, one that was intended to transform the Alexanderplatz into a thriving metropolis of the future.

The avant-garde office blocks that rose from the square were part of a competition-winning design submitted by renowned architect Peter Behrens. In his plans Behrens rejected the caryatids, Romanesque columns and scrollwork long favoured by city architects, viewing them as inherently pretentious and dishonest. His minimalist style was characteristic of the International Modern movement that began before World War I but was later reflected in many progressive buildings that went up in Berlin throughout the Weimar years.

Behrens took advantage of the latest construction techniques of steel reinforced concrete to turn his angular designs into reality. For both the Alexander Haus and Berolina Haus, he chose an exterior of double-square concrete panels with granite facing. This pattern was carried forward to each window, which was further subdivided into four square panes. Two identical eight-storey glazed staircases, brilliantly illuminated with neon lighting by night, completed the linear effect.

The ground floors of both buildings were reserved for retail use, while the upper storeys provided office space. Berolina Haus also housed the Berolina Rooftop Garden on its uppermost floor. Throughout the 1930s, this restaurant and dance hall became one of the most popular nightspots in central Berlin.

Much of Behrens' legacy on the Alexanderplatz was spared during the war. Its survival was all the more remarkable as the complex stood next to the strategic Alexanderplatz railway station. In one night alone, February 26th, 1944, Allied bombers saturated the area around the station with an estimated 2,796 tons of explosives.

*Opposite: Cabaret programme and night view of the Alexander Haus and Berolina Haus in the late 1930s. To the right stands the recently-"Aryanised" Hermann Tietz department store*

*Below: The Alexanderplatz Bahnhof in 1932, flanked by the Alexander Haus (left) and the Berolina Haus (right)*

*Damaged corner of the Alexander Haus in 1945*

After the war, huge crudely constructed posters of Stalin and Marshal Zhukov were erected on the square to remind Berliners of their new Soviet masters. Russian military police stood nearby directing traffic with their little flags while Trümmerfrauen (rubble women) sorted and stacked bricks from the neighbouring ruins of the Tietz department store. These women worked long, exhausting hours, but received extra food rations for their effort. Just three weeks after the last desperate battle, they had cleared most of the rubble away. Virtually every building around the square was subsequently levelled, but Behrens's masterpieces were spared. A restoration project returned the buildings to active service by 1952.

Prefabricated monstrosities like Josef Kaiser's Centrum department store and Heinz Mehlan's Haus der Elektroindustrie that went up on the Alexanderplatz a decade later made Behrens's minimalist office blocks seem almost quaint in comparison. The architect in charge of the overall development scheme, Joachim Näther, aimed for a "modern, international look", accenting the barren square with a few stylised frescoes and iron-work. That fabulous piece of GDR kitsch, the aluminium and enamel Urania World Time Clock (Urania-Weltzeituhr), dates from this era.

Restoration of Haus Alexander was initiated after unification and subsequently completed on November 15th, 1995. Now a protected landmark, the office building is currently occupied by its anchor tenant, the Bankgesellschaft Berlin. The recent glut of office space in central Berlin has delayed the restoration of Haus Berolina into the 21st century.

*Right: Peter Behrens' office blocks as they appeared during the early years of the GDR*

*Below: View of the Alexanderplatz in winter 2000, showing restoration work on the long-neglected Berolina Haus at its early stage*

# SHELL HAUS

*Opposite: Shell Haus under construction, winter 1931. Its unconventional design compelled the architect to visit city building authorities an astonishing 324 times before the project could be completed*

In the last days of the Weimar Republic, the Shell Oil Company commissioned Emil Fahrenkamp to design the headquarters for its German subsidiary, the Rhenania-Ossac-Gesellschaft. What resulted was one of the most important architectural projects to emerge from the inter-war years. Fahrenkamp, who was well known for his bold, industrial designs, called for a steel framed structure rather than one of poured concrete. His innovative approach also featured alternating waves of ribbon-like windows and limestone cladding, one that forced the exasperated architect to visit the city's building authorities no less than 324 times before his project could be completed.

Shell employees had to vacate their offices in 1940 to make way for bureaucrats of the German navy. Although Shell Haus managed to miraculously avoid destruction during the heavy air raids on the area, particularly those that levelled most of the neighbourhood in the late fall of 1943, its office workers were nevertheless affected by the deteriorating conditions of wartime Berlin. Ruined gas and power lines meant that navy functionaries were often obliged to work without electricity or heat in the dead of winter. With no light to work under, they would often find their workday shortened to end at 3 p.m. after the brief winter sun had set.

Its travertine façade was badly damaged by Russian heavy artillery during their final assault on the city, but Shell Haus emerged from the war more or less intact.

In November of 1945, the city's shattered diplomatic corps regrouped in the office tower while they waited for their ravaged embassies to be rebuilt or relocated. Three years later, it was the turn of BEWAG, Berlin's electric utility, to occupy Fahrenkamp's landmark building. There they would remain until 1995.

Shell Haus underwent major interior repairs in 1952 and had its outer surface covered in aluminium in 1960, but by the mid-1990s the

*Emil Fahrenkamp's finished product,*
*the Shell Haus next to Landwehr Canal*

*Above right: Shell Haus in May 1945, showing the holes made by Stalin's artillery during the Red Army's final assault on the city*

*Below right: Scaffolding clings to the ribbon-like façade of Shell Haus. Efforts have been made to restore many of the original details to this heritage building*

ten-storey structure had once again fallen into decline. After BEWAG
moved its offices to the south-east suburb of Treptow, the building — now
designated a protected monument — was left unoccupied.

Following "intense but constructive" negotiations with the city authorities, BEWAG in 1997 embarked on a renovation scheme that had the
derelict building stripped down to its skeleton for its most complete
restoration yet.

The badly-needed repairs that ultimately cost its owner 50 million DM
tried to balance the needs of future tenants with the preservation of
Fahrenkamp's original design. The building's crumbling exterior was
updated with panels of natural stone and its corroded steel window
frames were refitted in bronze. Inside, old wall partitions, sealed up light
wells and other sins of the 1950s were rectified. The large entrance hall,
staircases, skylights and distinctive steel doors were also returned to
their original state.

Berlin's gas utility, GASAG, has since moved into Fahrenkamp's building. A long-term leasing agreement will make Shell Haus the utility's headquarters for at least the next 10 years.

# COLUMBUS HAUS

Few places in Berlin have witnessed as many dramatic events this century as the narrow slice of land at the south-east corner of the Tiergarten known as the Lenné Triangle, between Bellevuestrasse and Königgrätzer Strasse.

Originally part of the King's hunting grounds, this parcel of land served as a school garden from 1750 right up to the mid-19th century. But as time went on and Berlin prospered, the school's mulberry plantations were divided up and replaced with high-density apartment blocks and retail storefronts.

In 1888, a six-storey hotel rose on the triangle's south-east corner, where the Bellevuestrasse and Königgrätzer Strasse met. Built by Ludwig Heim, the Bellevue Hotel faced its mirror image, the equally grand Palast directly across the street. For the next forty years, the two hotels would stand like identical Wilhelmine bookends at the north end of the square, welcoming the flood of travellers who poured out of the Potsdam railway terminus at all hours of the day.

By 1928, the Bellevue had fallen on hard times and was subsequently demolished to make way for a new development to be managed by Les Galleries Lafayette, a French retail chain. Financing for the project abruptly collapsed due in part to the effects of the Great Depression, which prompted the architect, Erich Mendelsohn, to erect a huge billboard over the idle construction site. Advertising revenue generated by the board helped his clients muster their finances for a continuation of the project.

Eventually, construction resumed and by mid-January 1933 the building officially opened, making Columbus Haus the last pre-war addition to the Potsdamer Platz.

Mendelsohn executed his modernist design using the latest advances in building technology. Cantilevered, poured-concrete supports were set

*Left: The Bellevue Hotel and the Palast at the north end of the Potsdamer Platz in 1910. The two hotels, with their identical mansard roofs and late Second Empire ornamentation, stood for 35 years on opposite sides of the Königgrätzer Strasse*

*Above: Billboards mask the stalled Columbus Haus project. Shortly after this photo was taken in 1931, financing was obtained and construction of Erich Mendelsohn's masterpiece began*

*Below: The completed Columbus Haus a few years later.*
*The office tower opened in the midst of a crippling world-wide depression.*
*Nonetheless, Mendelsohn's project soon attracted a prestige tenant —*
*a Woolworth department store on the main floor*

back into the building, allowing for its distinctive rooftop canopy and column-free plate glass façade. In the opinion of many, the curvilinear, clean lines that resulted made Mendelsohn's creation the finest example of the New Building (Neues Bauen) movement to be found in Berlin.

The next challenge for the owners of Columbus Haus was to find suitable tenants. Demand for retail space had plummeted by 40% since the derelict Bellevue hotel was first knocked down, and the effects of the Depression still lingered. Nonetheless, the prestigious allure of Mendelsohn's masterpiece gave the Columbus Haus an edge over its competition, prompting the F.W. Woolworth Company to sign a lease for the ground floor.

Intended as just one of many futuristic office towers to eventually surround the Potsdamer Platz, Mendelsohn's ten-storey creation was destined to have a short but eventful life. Its opening month coincided with the Nazi party's ascension to power and Mendelsohn's flight from Germany with his family. The Jewish architect would spend the rest of his life in exile.

Although Russian artillery fire had demolished the building's interior during the last days of the war, the Columbus Haus exterior miraculously withstood the more serious effects of aerial bombardment, attesting to Mendelsohn's sound building design and a good deal of luck. Shortly after the Nazi defeat, the lower floor of the Columbus Haus was renovated and subsequently occupied by the Wertheim department store and a few other commercial tenants. Meanwhile, the cold north German wind

*Opposite: Citizens and members of the Volkssturm (civil defence) erect tank barricades in front of Columbus Haus in late April 1945, during a last-ditch attempt to repel the Red Army*

*Below: As part of East Berlin, Columbus Haus became a tool in the propaganda war that raged between East and West Berlin. This photo shows the Columbus Haus bedecked with socialist slogans in August, 1951*

continued to whistle through the blackened girders of the building's exposed upper floors.

Division of Berlin into Russian, American, British, and French sectors of occupation was largely along the lines of pre-war parish boundaries, which sometimes made for strange results. One of these geographic oddities involved the Lenné Triangle, which now placed the Columbus Haus on a strip of Soviet-controlled land that jutted deep into the British sector.

Inevitably, the businesses that had slowly been taking root in the Columbus Haus after the war were confiscated by the East German state after the communist regime's founding in 1949. Wertheim was transformed into a government-run consumer goods outlet, joining a garage and a restaurant under communist administration. Meanwhile, as Berlin's political rivalry heated up, the structure's still-abandoned upper floors became festooned with vibrant messages of socialist goodwill and denunciations of the imperialist West.

The East German workers' revolt of 1953 sealed the fate of the Columbus Haus forever. The state-run shops on the ground floor were torched by enraged protesters, and the damage was never repaired. Shortly afterwards, the East German government chose to write off the building entirely. In 1956, crews began dismantling the structure floor by floor, removing what steel and other scarce building materials they could salvage. The last vestiges of the Columbus Haus disappeared in 1961 prior to the erection of the Berlin Wall.

When the time came to seal off the border, GDR security planners chose to abandon the Lenné Triangle by building the concrete barrier along its eastern face, down the Ebertstrasse. For years, this 10-acre wedge of land was effectively stateless.

In 1988, the West Berlin Senate finally acquired the land after trading it for a few irregular scraps of territory elsewhere on the city's western

perimeter. The idea was to build an expressway that would better connect the city's southern districts with Moabit and Wedding to the north. These plans were strongly opposed by environmentalists, who set up tents in the weed-filled lot in protest.

When the transfer was finally carried out on July 1st, the West Berlin police moved in to break up the camp. To avoid arrest, a number of supporters of the Green party and anarchists climbed over the Wall in what must have been the only reverse exodus of escapees in the barrier's 27-year history.

Berlin's reunification less than two years later prompted city authorities to rethink their road-building plans. The private banking firm of Delbrück and Co. has since acquired the portion of the Lenné Triangle once occupied by the Columbus Haus and commissioned architect Hans Kollhoff to draw up plans for a 70 million DM residential and commercial office tower.

A green wedge next to the Delbrück building will begin with its narrowest point south at the Potsdamer Platz and radiate out to the Tiergarten, adding a much needed bit of greenery to the crowded square.

*Above: Proposed successor to the Columbus Haus, the 17-storey Delbrück building*

*Opposite: View south of the planned Delbrück building. To the right is the Sony Center tower during its final phase of construction*

# WINTERGARTEN

To meet a growing demand for luxury accommodation in the rapidly-expanding metropolis of Berlin, businessman Hermann Geber opened the Central Hotel just south of the Friedrichstrasse railway station in 1880. Seven years later, Geber converted the hotel's glass-covered palm court into what was soon to become Berlin's most popular variety theatre, the Wintergarten.

Geber replaced the palm court's glazed roof with a ceiling of plaster, then had it painted blue and decorated with a thousand light bulbs, creating a kitschy night sky that would become the Wintergarten trademark. Patrons seated on a broad wine terrace to the rear of the auditorium could enjoy the revue's Vaudeville acts while dining on food brought in from the hotel's restaurant.

The Wintergarten quickly gained a reputation as one of the most prestigious night spots in Europe, thanks to its imaginative director, Julius Baron. Over the years the impresario would sign on a bizarre range of entertaining spectacles which, on a typical night, might include Chinese jugglers, a man eating dinner from a heavily-laden table while on a tightrope, cyclists on tall seats, and sultry chanteuses like "The Great Otero".

In 1895, Wintergarten representatives knew they were onto something big when heard about three Pankow inventors who had just created something called a "Bioscope", a machine that was supposed to make pictures move. On November 1st of that year, history was made when Max Skladanowsky demonstrated his invention at the Wintergarten — two months before the Lumière brothers made their own cinematic début in Paris. With Skladanowsky at the controls of his double projector, the audience was treated to several brief film clips of jugglers, Italian peasant dancers, and boxing kangaroos.

Another oddity to appear on the Wintergarten stage was an act by an American called Erich Weisse. Better known as Harry Houdini, he amazed

*Above left: The Central Hotel's palm court, which would soon be converted into Berlin's most popular variety theatre*

*Above right: View of the Wintergarten before its 1928 renovation. All women not seated in the loges or wine terrace were asked to remove their hats*

*Right: Martha Western's "Living Art" (Lebende Bilder) which appeared on the Wintergarten stage in 1925. At the time, city authorities tolerated public nudity as long as the "artists" remained motionless*

*Below: 1930s view of the Central Hotel at the corner of the Friedrichstrasse and Dorotheenstrasse. The main entrance to the Wintergarten was just around the corner to the left*

Wintergarten audiences by his ability to release himself from locked coils of heavy chains while submerged in a large tank of water.

After World War I, the number of visitors started to decline. Black pages in gold braid were still on hand to open the front doors, and the crowds continued to down cold beer in front of trapeze artists, near-naked dancers and other popular acts.

But increasingly, Berliners out for what they called "Amüsemang" headed for the neon lights of the New West End around the Zoo station. Inevitably, the huge La Scala on the Lutherstrasse replaced the Wintergarten as Berlin's premier revue.

In the early 1930s, Adolf Hitler could sometimes be seen in the audiences of the Wintergarten. He enjoyed its variety shows immensely, but once he became Chancellor he felt his presence was no longer appropriate. Sometimes he would send his house steward to the show with orders to return with a copy of the evening's programme and a full report of what he had seen that night.

In 1940, the Wintergarten enjoyed a brief renaissance. As the battles across Europe dragged on and rationing grew ever tighter, variety shows were one of the few things left for Berliners to spend their money on. But the shows themselves were increasingly difficult to produce due to the mounting restrictions on what was acceptable for public entertainment. American jazz and blues, while tremendously popular, were already taboo. Then, in 1941, the ever-popular fortune tellers, hypnotists and mind-readers were outlawed because Joseph Goebbels feared their

*A ruined portion of the Central Hotel and Wintergarten entrance after the war*

growing influence over the public. (It was rumoured that Rudolf Heß fell under the spell of one of these mystics and was persuaded to make his ill-fated trip to Scotland.) That left Wintergarten to fill the gap with a mediocre assortment of torch singers, acrobats and jugglers.

Heavy fighting on the Friedrichstrasse in the last days of the war helped to destroy the last traces of the Central Hotel and its Wintergarten stage.

In one of its last urban initiatives before its demise, the East German regime sought to transform the Friedrichstrasse into a shopping and entertainment hub that would rival the Kurfürstendamm in the West. The plan spawned a number of building projects here in the mid-1980s, including the Friedrichstrasse Arcades, the Grand Hotel, and the Friedrich-stadtpalast. A new entertainment complex was also envisaged to replace the Central Hotel's long-departed Wintergarten at its original site on the corner of the Dorotheenstrasse. One government publication issued in 1987 optimistically predicted that "…in the near future the site will once again be offering hours of fun as a variety revue."

The collapse of the communist regime 24 months later put paid to any such state-sponsored entertainment. Plans now exist for the vacant site to be converted into offices for the ZDF television network.

The Wintergarten tradition remains alive and well on the Potsdamer Strasse. The new Wintergarten revue remains a popular venue for visitors and locals who wish to relive the glory days of Berlin's variety theatre.

The gap left by the Central Hotel south of the
Friedrichstrasse railway station has served as
green space for over 50 years. At present,
the "Friedrich-Carré" will be built there

# NOLLENDORFPLATZ THEATRE

At the time of modern Germany's founding, what is now Berlin's Schöneberg district was a small town of 4,500 inhabitants separated from neighbouring villages by fields of rye and potatoes. But within a few short years, all this would change. Five billion marks in war reparations from the French government and a wildly surging stock market helped fuel a building boom in the West End that saw land prices rise by 600 percent between 1871 and 1874. Landowners who had for years eked out a modest existence on their farms sold their fields and became instant millionaires. Their land was divided up, roads were put through and in no time five- and six-storey housing developments were going up all over the place. By 1898, Schöneberg had blossomed into a district of 100,000 souls.

In the middle of all this was the thousand-seat Nollendorfplatz Theatre. Built in 1906 to entertain Schöneberg's burgeoning population, it initially staged a variety of light operettas, chiefly in the summer months. After a period of decline, the theatre was given a new lease on life in 1927 with the arrival of 34-year-old Erwin Piscator.

Piscator was a mercurial spirit who had tried for years to arouse Berlin's revolutionary spirit through his avant-garde stage productions. His last directorship was at the Volksbühne, which he left after a dispute with the management. After having received backing from the wealthy husband of actress Tilla Durieux, Piscator debuted here on the Nollendorfplatz with Ernst Toller's "Hoppla, wir leben noch" (Hooray, We're Still Alive). The production featured a film projector showing newsreels of marching revolutionaries and a multi-level set fashioned out of steel beams. This was Piscator's classic approach to "Epic Theatre", a combination of politics and technology whose purpose was "to learn how to think, rather than how to feel." The play was an instant hit.

Emboldened by his success, Piscator continued to provide more scandalously entertaining plays to Berlin audiences. His production of

*Opposite: Oskar Karlweiss and Lizzi Waldmüller in "Traum einer Nacht" which premièred at the Nollendorfplatz Theatre in 1930. By then, Piscator was no longer directing at the theatre*

*Below: The Nollendorfplatz Theatre in 1927, the year when the fiery Erwin Piscator opened his experimental Piscatorbühne. His controversial plays soon became the toast of the town*

Alexei Tolstoy's Rasputin prompted a lawsuit from the exiled Kaiser. Another play, "The Good Soldier Schweik", contained an inflammatory set design by artist George Grosz that included a crucified Christ wearing army boots and a gas mask. The wealthy élite of Weimar Berlin flocked to the next Piscator production, paying exorbitant prices for opening night seats and a chance to witness Berlin's next scandal.

On the eve of the Great Depression in 1929, Piscator opened "Der Kaufmann von Berlin". The play was about a poor East European Jew who arrived in Berlin during the inflationary chaos of the early 20s and, through serendipity, became a multi-millionaire. The play offended some of the wealthier members of the audience on its opening night, prompting the management to remove Piscator's name from the theatre marquee and ban him from the premises.

Soon afterward, the playhouse continued operating solely as a movie theatre. In December 1930, the famous anti-war movie "All Quiet on the Western Front" was screened in the Mozart Hall. Police officers had to forcibly restrain crowds of Nazi thugs who gathered in the square outside to discourage the public from watching such a "defeatist" film. Once the movie began, a few troublemakers snuck into the darkened salon to let off stink bombs and release a small army of white mice.

After the war, the neighbourhood around the Nollendorfplatz maintained its pre-war reputation for seediness, and the rebuilt Hall operated in its midst as a pornographic theatre. In 1978, the auditorium was redecorated with glitter balls and flashing lights to open as a New York-style disco. The old theatre continues to serve as one of Berlin's largest discotheques.

*A 1920s postcard showing the theatre's interior garden court*

*Opposite above: The damaged garden court in 1944*

*Below: The building (today Metropol) continues as a place of raucous entertainment. Playbills on its front doors advertise a new generation's music of groove, hip hop and "funky jazzy stuff"*

# VOLKSBÜHNE

Before the advent of blockbuster American films and cable television, many Berliners turned to the stage for their entertainment. In fact, a controversial new play in the 1920s would arouse a passion that would surprise many of us today: it had the power to provoke spirited debates at dinner tables and cafés across the city. In many cases, the imaginatively written and brilliantly designed productions in Berlin's thirty-five serious theatres acted as a safety valve for a public rocked by the political and social turbulence of the inter-war years.

The Volksbühne theatre company, which staged its first play in 1890, owed its phenomenal success to its low subscription fees and high-quality productions. It offered an alternative to the conservative, state-sponsored theatre and opera houses that dominated the city at the time. At 50 pfennigs a ticket, its plays were accessible to all but the most impoverished residents of Berlin's east end. Though the theatre was run by conservative business interests, its productions were strongly influenced by the German Socialist Party, and operated in the tradition of workers' theatre groups.

The theatre company's playhouse was built on the Bülowplatz in 1913, at a time when the number of subscribers approached an impressive 30,000. The first manager of the new theatre was celebrated director Max Reinhardt. He oversaw its productions between 1915 and 1918 before moving on to create his remarkable theatre in the round at the old Schumann Circus on the Schiffbauerdamm.

Naturalist plays by Ibsen and Gerhart Hauptmann had long since been the mainstays of the Volksbühne, but these more sedate productions ended with the arrival of Erwin Piscator. He appeared in 1924 to direct "Fahnen", a political epic that chronicled the anarchist riots in Chicago. Piscator had a penchant for combining his plays with mechanical devices like moving platforms and treadmills that were designed to stimulate the

*Above left: Theatre programme from the days when the Volksbühne was obliged to obey the dictates of Joseph Goebbels' Propaganda Ministry*

*Above right: Heinrich George (right) and Erwin Kaiser in Erwin Piscator's production of "Gewitter über Gotland" at the Volksbühne*

*Below: The Volksbühne on the Bülowplatz,*
*designed by architect Oskar Kaufmann and*
*built in 1913*

audience and compete with the increasingly popular phenomenon of moving pictures.

Piscator's next production was "Sturmflut", a thriller set during the Russian Revolution. In it, he had film clips of naval battles and crowd scenes projected in the background as "a piece of living scenery." But, despite his best efforts, Piscator's plays never achieved the runaway success he had hoped for. He left the Volksbühne and headed across town to the Nollendorfplatz, following a dispute with management over a play called "Die Wandlung". The playhouse owner felt it was too radical for their audience and refused to allow Piscator to put it on.

Situated in the heart of the working class Scheunenviertel district, the Volksbühne was the scene of a real-life drama in August 1931 when the biggest street brawl since the Spartakist revolts of 1919 erupted on its doorstep. Some blamed the communists for creating a disturbance that ultimately saw over a thousand Berliners take part, while others said they were provoked into violence by the police. When the riot finally ended, two policemen lay dead and the nearby Communist Party headquarters had been ransacked. Less than a year later, such scenes would disappear, as the pall of Nazi "law and order" descended over the city.

Shortly thereafter, the Volksbühne was forced into bankruptcy by the Berlin municipal government and subsequently reopened under the auspices of Joseph Goebbels' Ministry of Public Enlightenment and Propaganda. Gone were Piscator's wild experiments: all plays after 1933 would now have to meet the stringent approval of Nazi censors.

After the war, the Soviet occupiers looked favourably upon the ruined Volksbühne and its working class roots. They helped to reopen the theatre that had been completely gutted after a November 20th, 1943, air raid. By providing extra rations to all writers, artists and playwrights who produced work that promoted "socialist reality", the Soviets ensured that many a politically correct production was staged at the Volksbühne, especially during the lean years of 1945-46.

Shortly before his death in the late 1960s, the controversial Piscator briefly returned to his old playhouse to direct Truman Capote's documentary classic "In Cold Blood". The play's portrayal of random violence in the American Midwest fit perfectly with the communist belief of Western society's imminent collapse.

Today the Volksbühne remains one of the more interesting and affordable of Berlin's theatrical venues. Audiences who attend productions by current director Frank Castorf can expect controversy, nudity, and, from time to time, objects thrown at them from the stage.

The Volksbühne after the war.
Between 1952 and 1954, reconstruction of
the theatre's interior reduced the seating
capacity from 2000 to a more intimate 849

Behind its simplified exterior, the
Volksbühne continues to provide lively
entertainment to all who pass through
its doors

# ADMIRALSPALAST

In 1911, an enormous entertainment complex opened just north of the Friedrichstrasse railway station on the foundations of the old Admirals-gartenbad. In addition to a luxury swimming pool, skating rink, and res-taurant, the new Admiralspalast offered Berliners something unusual: a movie theatre. A few cramped and dingy screening rooms were already operating in various parts of the city, but now for the first time audiences could enjoy the comfort and clear sightlines of a modern-style cinema auditorium. Its plush surroundings attracted a more upscale crowd, help-ing to give Berlin's movie-going experience a greater respectability. Within a few years, a spate of extravagantly-designed cinemas began popping up elsewhere, particularly around the Kurfürstendamm in the New West End.

In 1922, the ice rink was replaced with another auditorium so that the Admiralspalast could join its competitors, the Renaissance and the Trian-on, to stage another equally popular form of entertainment, the variety revue.

Throughout the "Golden Twenties", the Admiral Girls kicked up their heels nightly in glittering extravaganzas on the Admiralspalast stage. With nudity being an essential feature of these shows, they offered pay-ing customers a titillating chorus line of legs, feathers and top hats. Like the Tiller Girls, the Paris Mannequins, and other troupes of scantily-clad dancers, their rigidly-choreographed numbers evoked the promise of a new and rational age. In the words of reviewer Siegfried Kracauer, "every girl's leg is one thirty-secondth of a marvellously precise machine… A button is pressed and the girl contraption cranks into motion, perform-ing impressively at thirty-two horsepower." Industrial psychologist Fritz Giese coined the term "Girlkultur" to describe this phenomenon of regimented titillation.

The popularity of the revue in the 20s mirrored the emerging prosperity of Berlin, a time when the city offered a choice of over 16,000 bars, cafés

*Above left: The Admiralspalast's gilded loges following a renovation project by Kaufmann and Wolffenstein in 1930*

*Above right: The Art Deco cloakroom after its 1930 facelift*

*Opposite: The 2,200-seat Admiralspalast just north of the Friedrichstrasse railway station in 1928. Two doors down the street is the rounded Neo-Baroque façade of the Komische Oper*

*Opposite: Nudity was an essential feature of the Admiralspalast's popular "Haller Revue". Here the revue girls drape themselves over a replica of the Brandenburg Gate's Quadriga in 1926*

*Below: The front of the Admiralspalast littered with wrecked military vehicles just days before the Nazi surrender*

and dance halls. But the Admiralspalast's star began to fade a decade later when, in growing numbers, Berliners turned to escapist movies for diversion from the joblessness and social unrest that started to plague their daily existence. The glamour and promise of the elaborately-staged variety show somehow seemed passé. Increasingly, the Admiralspalast relied on upbeat musical productions to fill its seats.

The first bomb of World War II to fall on the Admiralspalast struck on April 9th, 1941, but damage was relatively light and performances continued after a brief hiatus. Three years later, Joseph Goebbels ordered the establishment to shut its doors, as part of a wartime edict that closed theatres and other entertainment venues city-wide. Disaster struck the empty theatre on February 3rd, 1945, when the Admiralspalast suffered three direct hits by incendiary bombs. The attack completely gutted Kaufmann and Wolffenstein's gilded 1930s auditorium.

After peace had finally returned to the Friedrichstrasse in spring of 1945, the City Council determined that the Admiralspalast, though heavily-damaged, could nonetheless be salvaged. The cost of repairing the structure was eventually two million Reichmarks, far above its initial 650,000 mark estimate.

The Staatsoper ensemble, who were left homeless following the destruction of von Knobelsdorff's 18th century opera house on the Unter den Linden, moved into the tattered Admiralspalast in the fall of 1945. Here they remained under the direction of Ernst Legal until the mid-1950s, during which time they staged 59 productions that spanned over 1,100 performances. Their return to the rebuilt opera house in March of 1955 permitted the Metropol theatre troupe, who themselves had been displaced during the war, to take their place.

During these early post-war years, the Admiralspalast served not only as a venue for culture in the shattered city, it also bore witness to a forced political marriage engineered by the Soviets that would shape the future of divided Germany for the next 43 years. On April 21st, 1946, over a thousand delegates from the German Communist Party (KPD) and the Social Democratic Party (SPD) streamed into the Admiralspalast auditorium to the sounds of Beethoven's Fidelio overture. At 10 a.m. Wilhelm Pieck, leader of the KPD, crossed the stage to shake hands with his counterpart, Otto Grotewohl of the SPD, an act that signalled a merger of their respective parties into the Socialist Unity Party of Germany (SED). This historic handshake would soon turn into an iron fist.

The Admiralspalast went on to host musicals and stage productions throughout the 40-year lifespan of the East German regime. In a rare display of tolerance the communists also permitted East Berlin's only permanent cabaret, Die Distel (The Thistle), to open in 1953. It became one of the few places in the GDR where comedians could get up on stage and make fun of SED party leaders and their policies without fear of reprisal. The Distel's manager, Otto Stark, insisted that while his cabaret may, from time to time, have poked fun at official narrow-mindedness, under no circumstances did he ever allow it to degenerate into "an outlet for petty bourgeois grumbling or a know-it-all attitude."

Today, the Admiralspalast is witnessing a revival of the long-dormant Friedrichstrasse and remains home to both its historic cabaret and the recently-privatised Metropol theatrical troupe.

# KROLL OPERA HOUSE

The original Kroll establishment appeared in 1844 after Joseph Kroll, an entrepreneur from Breslau, secured royal assent to open a "winter garden" in the former exercise grounds near the Brandenburg Gate. Kroll's sprawling pleasure garden and dance complex grew over the years to encompass 27 halls that could accommodate an impressive 5000 guests.

Four years after it opened, the Kroll began playing host to a series of operatic performances. A newer and grander opera house opened half a century later, in 1898, and went on to host a variety of memorable events under the direction of Jacob Karl Engel, including the first performance of Wagner's "Tannhäuser" in Berlin. Formerly managed by the same organisation that ran the Volksbühne, ownership was transferred to the Prussian state government after the opera house ran into financial troubles. Throughout the Weimar years, the 2000-seat playhouse became the scene of publicly subsidised entertainment.

In 1927, a young man called Otto Klemperer arrived from Cologne to become the musical director of the Kroll Opera House. Radical, short-tempered, but with a genius for innovation, Klemperer assumed almost dictatorial powers. Under his direction, the Kroll became known as a venue for performances of modern musical compositions by Paul Hindemith, Igor Stravinsky and Arnold Schönberg, in addition to its regular performances of such classical greats as Madame Butterfly and Carmen. Abetted by his team of modernist colleagues, including designer Ewald Duelberg and dramaturge Hans Curjel, even the most traditional of orchestral pieces were subject to radical sets and unknown musical scores. Klemperer's unorthodox interpretation of Richard Wagner's "Flying Dutchman" prompted Wagner's son Siegfried to shout "Cultural bolshevism!" from his seat. Another of Klemperer's productions that raised conservative eyebrows was Paul Hindemith's "Neues vom Tage". Here, the director had the soprano sing from a bathtub.

*Opposite: Otto Klemperer (right) seated next to Igor Stravinsky, 1928. During his tenure as musical director at the Kroll, Klemperer both inspired and scandalised his audiences with his avant-garde productions*

*Above right: The Kroll Opera House on the Königsplatz in the Tiergarten, circa 1920*

*Below right: Seriously damaged during the bitter fighting that preceded the fall of Berlin, the Kroll Opera House was finally pulled down in 1951. This photo shows the Kroll in 1946, its garden restaurant for the moment still bravely carrying on*

Mirroring the growing conservatism that had begun to creep in during the last days of the Weimar Republic, the Prussian state government grew increasingly impatient with Klemperer's quirky avant-garde style. One nationalist member of the Landtag accused the Kroll of becoming a purveyor of "nigger culture". Public funding of Kroll performances was abruptly cut off in 1930 in the face of soaring deficits. For a time, the performances continued, with Leoš Janáček's "House of the Dead" opening in May 1931, but deprived of its annual 1.8 million mark subsidy the historic opera house was forced to close soon afterwards. Klemperer himself fled Germany in 1933.

After the Reichstag building directly across the Königsplatz burned down in 1933, the Kroll auditorium served as the meeting point for Germany's parliamentarians. However, with Adolf Hitler pulling all the levers of power legislative proceedings became a farce. Despite an early display of protest by the socialist deputies, parliamentary delegates were bullied into approving whatever laws were put before them, most notably the Enabling Law which gave the Nazis complete freedom to do whatever they wanted to their opponents. In its nine years of existence, the members of the Reichstag met at the Kroll building precisely 18 times.

The structure was used as an artillery stronghold during the last-ditch defence of the area around the Reichstag and, as a result, was heavily damaged. A remnant continued to function as a café after the war, but on March 27th, 1951, it was demolished. Today, there remains not a trace of the old opera house. Over one hundred and fifty years after the construction of the first Kroll establishment here in 1844, the site has reverted to its original state — a field of grass.

*Opera house no longer: the music of Stravinsky at the Kroll*
*has now been replaced with the warbling of finches*
*in the Tiergarten*

# RATHAUS BRIDGE

The first bridge to cross this part of the River Spree was erected in 1300, at a time when Berlin had only begun to shed its past as an unimportant cross-roads on the sandy Brandenburg plains. Crudely fashioned of logs from nearby forests, the original wooden span was known as the Long Bridge and joined the settlement of Berlin on the east side of the river to the town of Cölln to the west. A few years later, a crude wooden Rathaus, or town hall, was built right on the bridge. Here, suspended in neutral territory over the water, representatives from Berlin and Cölln could meet to address common issues.

As Berlin grew in importance, the Long Bridge became part of the ceremonial route for visiting royalty and guests to the Imperial Palace. The top photo in the sequence on the opposite page shows the palace behind the bridge as it looked between the two world wars. Directly behind the bridge's middle arch was the palace garden, beyond which stood the corner turrets that dated back to 1580. These copper-topped turrets were sometimes referred to as the "green hats" or "pepper pots" and formed one of the oldest parts of the city castle. To the right in the distance is the massive Neo-Baroque dome of the Berlin Cathedral.

The original wooden span had many replacements over the next four centuries, but in 1695, a more permanent stone bridge was erected. Inspired by the famous Pont-Neuf of Paris, its five-arched design influenced royal attempts at bridge building for the next 100 years. In the summer of 1703, a balcony was added midway across the span to accommodate a statue of the Great Elector, the Hohenzollern prince who rescued Berlin from the agony of the Thirty Years' War. The monument was executed by Andreas Schlüter, the same architect who participated in the reconstruction of the neighbouring palace. The completed sculpture had four bronze figures chained to a corner of the marble plinth, depicting the craven subjects of his various military conquests. From this time

*A pre-war view of the Kurfürsten Bridge.*
*In the centre of the span is Andreas*
*Schlüter's monument to the Great Elector.*
*The oldest part of the Imperial Palace can*
*be seen directly behind the sculpture*

*The shattered bridge in 1946. By then,*
*Schlüter's statue was sitting on a barge*
*farther downstream at the Borsig Docks*

*Today, the Palace of the Republic*
*dominates the view of the bridge*

onward, the span came to be known as the Kurfürsten Bridge.

World War II left the Kurfürsten Bridge in a sad state of disrepair. As the Russians drew nearer to Berlin, a decision was taken to dismount the Great Elector from his vantage point on the bridge and remove him to a place of safety. A barge was dispatched to collect Schlüter's masterpiece and soon the monument was securely placed on board. The boat cast off for its journey down the Spree, ultimately docking downriver at the Borsig Docks. There the Great Elector sat until 1947, when his overloaded barge finally sank. The bronze statue remained in the river's murky black waters for two years before it was retrieved and placed in front of the Charlottenburg Palace. It remains there to this day.

As the Battle for Berlin reached its climax, Wehrmacht sappers destroyed the westernmost span of the Kurfürsten Bridge in a last ditch attempt to slow the advancing Red Army. After the war, the span was crudely mended with a few steel beams and covered in wooden planks.

Today, the old bridge has a drably functional replacement, complete with exposed gas pipes running along its underside. It continues to go by its communist-era name, the Rathaus Bridge, in honour of the ancient town hall that was once suspended over these waters.

# OBERBAUM BRIDGE

The 150-metre long Oberbaum Bridge crosses the Spree at its widest point in central Berlin. Its name evokes a much earlier time when this part of the river was guarded by a floating customs gate of roughly-hewn timbers.

The two-level crossing was designed by Otto Stahn and completed in 1896. Its upper deck was built to accommodate the new municipal elevated railway while an arcaded pedestrian walkway and road on the lower level provided additional access for pedestrians and vehicular traffic. The bridge's Gothic brick exterior was quaint but deceptive; it hid a very modern structure of steel-reinforced concrete.

In the early photograph, directly behind the bridge's twin medieval-style towers, the German Incandescent Light Factory can faintly be seen in the distance. From the time of its founding in 1892, hundreds of workers would cross the Oberbaum Bridge from their homes in the Kreuzberg district and take their place on the factory's assembly lines making parts for gas lamps. In time, the neighbourhood north of the Oberbaum Bridge became known as the Lampenstadt, or Gas Lamp City. After 1909, the plant expanded into the manufacture of light bulbs under the Osram trademark.

Over time, the view of the light bulb factory became obscured by one of the massive refrigerated warehouses that went up on the northern bank of the Spree in the early part of the 20th century. During World War II, vast quantities of eggs and other perishable goods were stored in these enormous buildings and distributed in a strictly controlled rationing system. By April 23rd, 1945, however, the Russians had reached the city limits and it became obvious that the existing rationing system could no longer be maintained. That day, the vast food storage rooms were thrown open to the public, a move that prompted crowds of Berliners to surge across the Oberbaum Bridge, risking shellfire and bombs, to return laden down with sides of beef and eggs.

The Oberbaum Bridge shortly after its opening in 1896.
The span linked the northern industrial district of Friedrichshain
with the working class neighbourhood of Kreuzberg to the south

The conclusion of the Battle for Berlin left the Oberbaum Bridge relatively intact, with only the centre span breached. It was soon patched up and continued in its role as a commuter bridge. However, the industrial east bank now lay in Soviet hands and the workers' homes lay across the water in the American sector. Nevertheless, since Berlin was still considered an "open city", Berliners could cross the bridge as before, working by day in factories like the nationalised Osram factories in the East and sleeping at night in their homes in the West. On their way back over the bridge at the end of the day, workers would often be handed propaganda leaflets by East German agents, only to discard them once they had reached the American sector.

This free exchange of workers between the two halves of the city abruptly ended on August 13th, 1961, with the formal division of the city. After a temporary closure, the bridge reopened in 1972, but the Oberbaum Bridge was now restricted to Berlin citizens with proper special travel permits — foreigners, for example, had to cross farther west at Checkpoint Charlie on the Kochstrasse. A brick wall was built over the S-Bahn tracks and a concrete barricade blocked off road traffic. Despite these new restrictions, the Oberbaum Bridge became the most heavily-used transit point for locals travelling between East and West Berlin.

Today, the Oberbaum Bridge has been completely restored. Its decapitated towers were rebuilt between 1992 and 1995, the battered brickwork repointed and the S-Bahn links restored at a total cost of DM 70 million. A completely faithful reconstruction of Stahn's 1896 version was not possible, however. The centre arch remains slightly higher than the original span so that larger modern ships can pass beneath the bridge.

*The Oberbaum Bridge in 1961. It became an important transit point for West Berliners during Berlin's years of division*

*Opposite above: A Russian infantryman takes cover during the Red Army's assault on the bridge in late April, 1945*

*Above right: A view of the Oberbaum Bridge immediately after its capture by the Russians. One of the looted dockside warehouses can be seen in the background*

*Below right: The Oberbaum Bridge in 2000. The famous Berlin Bear has been added to the tip of the left tower*

# ANHALT STATION

On June 15th, 1880, Otto von Bismarck arrived at the Askanischer Platz to witness the grand opening of Berlin's newest and most majestic railway terminus yet, the Anhalt Station. The Reich Chancellor may have been struck by its sweeping 34-metre high concourse or its finely-detailed terra-cotta brickwork, but he had no love for the age of steam. "These railways," he huffed, "they only get in the way of traffic."

Bismarck's distaste for rail travel was very much misplaced: the new railhead he helped inaugurate was a vital transportation link to the Reich's rapidly-expanding capital. Just a few minutes' carriage ride to Prussia's administrative centre on the Wilhelmstrasse, the Anhalt Station was also in convenient proximity to the diplomatic quarter in the Tiergarten district and the great banking houses a few streets north on the Behrenstrasse.

Franz Schwechten's monumental terminus replaced a smaller structure that had been operating here since 1841, when a locomotive built by August Borsig first chugged its way to Jüterbog, 60 kilometres to the south. Now, in 1880, the rail network had grown to the point where trains leaving the Anhalt Station could take passengers as far as Dresden, with further connections to Prague, Vienna, Rome, and Athens.

Over the course of the next 72 years, trains pulling in to one of the station's six platforms would disgorge a litany of historic figures, from kings to revolutionaries. On May 21st, 1889, King Umberto I of Italy stepped off a new 400,000 mark train built in Florence expressly for his visit. The seven salon cars and two Pullman coaches that carried him over the Italian and Swiss Alps had made the entire journey in an impressive 41 hours. Emperor William II was on hand to greet him, dressed in a crisp white tunic and gleaming calf-length boots.

*Left: Loading of food hampers into a dining car at the Anhalt Station in 1930*

*Right: Train travellers were well served by numerous hotels in the area. This 1920s-era baggage sticker shows the Hotel Hollstein just east of the terminus. Note the hotel's actual size in the far left of the photo below*

*Below: The Anhalt Station on the south side of the Askanischer Platz in 1927. Built in 1880, at a cost of 6.9 million marks, it was at the time the largest train station in continental Europe*

During the golden age of the 1930s when rail travel was supreme, a train would arrive and depart under the terminal's cavernous glass atrium every three to five minutes, transporting an estimated 40,000 people every day. In 1930, 16 million train passengers stepped on or off a train at the Anhalt Station alone, compared to a mere 49,000 travellers who flew in and out of Tempelhof airport.

If the newly-arrived were not quite ready to face the bustling city, they could check in to one of a half dozen luxurious establishments that lay within a four-block radius of the station. They could book a room at the Hotel Hollstein next door at 38 Stresemannstrasse, or, after 1928, they could take a pedestrian tunnel that ran 100 metres below ground and ride an elevator directly up to the lobby of Kurt Elchner's gigantic Excelsior Hotel.

Like the Potsdam Station just 600 metres west of here, the Anhalt terminus would have been mothballed had Albert Speer's plan for the new Reich capital come to pass. By 1950, trains headed into the city from the south were to be diverted to a gigantic new rail terminal near Tempelhof. Once the new station became operational, Speer planned to convert the Anhalt terminus into a public swimming pool.

During the war, the historic railway station suffered repeated air attacks by British and American bombers. During the last days of the Battle of Berlin, a deadly duel between Wehrmacht sharpshooters and advancing Soviet troops played itself out in the burned-out terminal. Fighting stopped at 10 p.m. on April 30th, 1945, when the railway station fell to the Red Army.

In the years that followed, goods from the Siemens Works, the municipal electrical plant, various department stores, even movie studios were crated up and shipped to the Anhalt Station. Mountains of wooden containers stamped with Cyrillic lettering indicating destinations to Moscow, Odessa, Kharkov and points east collected on the platforms, waiting for trains that never came. The equipment lay abandoned because most of the railway tracks leading east had already been dismantled by the Soviets for scrap iron.

The rail network was eventually patched up and trains returned to the partially-ruined station, only to be diverted once again by order of the communist-controlled railway, the Reichsbahn. In May 1952, passenger trains from the south were permanently re-routed to the East Station in East Berlin as part of the GDR's ongoing effort to isolate the city's western sectors. Despite strong public opposition, the Anhalt Station was demolished eight years later.

Above right: The heavily damaged station two months after its capture by the Red Army in July, 1945

Opposite: Inside the terminus in 1947. The railway station remained in service until the communist-controlled Reichsbahn re-routed passenger trains to the east in 1952

Below right: Today, just a fragment of the old station's colonnaded portico remains. The sculpted figures of Day and Night remain at its summit, but the vintage electric clock that stood between them is long gone

# POTSDAM STATION

The first scheduled passenger service to operate in south-central of Berlin predated the steam engine by almost 150 years. In 1690, a mail coach to Leipzig passed through what is now the Potsdamer Platz, when the square was little more than sheep pasture at the south-west edge of the old city customs wall. The coach service improved over the years, but was regularly disrupted each spring when floods made nearby rivers impassable.

The introduction of the steam engine in the 1830s soon made long distance travel by horse-drawn coach obsolete. Recognising the military and commercial potential of this new invention, business interests founded the Berlin-Potsdam Railway Company (Berlin-Potsdam Eisenbahngesellschaft) and, in 1838, inaugurated Berlin's first rail line, a length of track that began at the Potsdamer Platz and stretched as far as Potsdam 26 kilometres to the south. Ten years later, the line was extended to Magdeburg, whose connections linked Berlin to Europe's rapidly-expanding rail network.

The German public embraced this new form of transportation with great enthusiasm. Within a few decades, as rail lines penetrated almost every corner of the Prussian kingdom, train travel became an inexpensive and extremely reliable way to cross great distances. To handle the growing number of rail passengers, a new terminus was erected on the south side of the Potsdamer Platz and dedicated in 1872. For the next fifty years, the flood of travellers who arrived at the Potsdam station from the four corners of the earth gave rise to a vibrant neighbourhood of luxury hotels, art galleries and fine restaurants.

In 1933, the newly-elected Adolf Hitler complained to the city mayor that Berlin was very "unsystematic", that its random, twisting streets did not fit his vision of Berlin as capital of a new world order. Albert Speer's model for a reorganised city, completed a few years later, called for the

*Opposite: Interior view of the busy terminal in 1932*

*Below: The Potsdam railway station on the south end of the Potsdamer Platz. In the foreground to the left is the old Trinity Parish cemetery. After the lease on the last grave expired in 1910, the cemetery was paved over*

Potsdam station to be abandoned. Rail traffic in Hitler's future metropolis would be diverted to two gigantic terminals, one at the north end and the other at the south end of the city.

Paradoxically, the invasion of Poland in 1939 gave the Potsdam station and the city's other railheads a temporary reprieve. Nazi authorities now spent their energy trying to protect their ageing terminals from Allied attack. At times, they resorted to devious methods like constructing "mirage" train stations out of nets and scaffolding in an attempt to redirect the falling bombs.

As the battles drew closer to the city, train travel became increasingly dangerous. By January 8th, 1945, trains leaving the Potsdam station bound for western German cities could travel only at night, when air attack was less likely. Two weeks later, even night travel could not be attempted. On the 23rd of January, the last civilian train of the war left the heavily-damaged station.

After the war, agreements between the western Allies and the Russians meant that the rail network serving Berlin, including the S-Bahn, would be administered by the communist-run Deutsche Reichsbahn (DR). This gave rise to an odd situation: the Potsdam tracks, together with those that led to all the other shattered railway stations in the British, French and American sectors, were now controlled by the East German state.

In 1946, the DR cleared a few lines leading out of the fire-scorched terminal, permitting limited travel to outlying areas. But in the early 1950s, the East German regime closed them down again under the excuse that they were trying to prevent American interference with inter-zonal rail traffic. Trains were now forced to pass through a few strictly controlled transit points. Left isolated and without a purpose, the Potsdam station was torn down in 1957.

After 1961, the newly-constructed Berlin Wall ran across the square in front of the recently-departed station. For the next 25 years or so, the scrubland south of the Wall became a neutral zone, serving at various times as a parking lot for itinerant caravans, a flea market and lovers' hideout.

The unexpected fall of the Berlin Wall instantly transformed the site into a building developer's dream. It also provoked a heated debate. Environmentalists, wanted the surroundings to be preserved as a green space, while commercial interests sought to turn the area into a consumer paradise of high-end boutiques and pricey condominiums.

*A ruined anti-aircraft gun sits among the detritus of war in front of the ruined station*

To help settle matters, the Berlin Senate invited urban planners and architects to participate in a competition that would propose a master plan for development of the Potsdamer Platz. The first prize was ultimately awarded to Munich architects Heinz Hilmer and Christoph Sattler.

Hilmer and Sattler's plan called for a low-rise development of commercial and residential buildings that would bring street life back to the square after all the years of division. One trap they wished to avoid was the creation of huge American-style indoor malls that tend to suck up pedestrians from the surrounding streets. Only time will tell what effect the many compromises later struck between Berlin's building authorities and the developers will have on Hilmer and Sattler's original vision.

One aspect of the Hilmer and Sattler plan that survived intact was the transformation of the Potsdam station site into a public park. Named after the popular actress who appeared on the Berlin stage in the early 20th century, the new Tilla Durieux Park is being preserved as a 2.5 hectare long avenue of greenery linking the Potsdamer Platz with the Landwehr Canal to the south. This "splendid track" is the product of Dutch landscape architects, Maike van Stiphout and Bruno Doedens.

*Opposite: View of the Potsdam station one year before its final demolition in 1957. The sector line dividing East Berlin from the American sector ran directly in front of the station's entrance*

*Below: The new regional railways station Potsdamer Platz. To the left the Park Kolonnaden, to the right the Daimler-Chrysler complex*

# LEHRTE STATION

Unlike the cities of Leipzig or Frankfurt on Main, Berlin never had a primary railway station at its core. The city was still bounded by an ancient customs wall in the 1830s and 40s when railway stations were first contemplated. As a result, a ring of lesser stations was built outside the old barricade in what was, at the time, the outskirts of town.

The first rail terminus to serve Germany's northern and western regions was the Hamburg Station, which opened just north of the Humboldt Docks in 1847. Less than a quarter century later, this rather plain-looking terminal was overshadowed by a much grander structure constructed just a few blocks to the south-west.

In 1871, trains travelling between Berlin and the cities of Hanover, Bremen and Hamburg were redirected to the newly-built Lehrte Station. Its Neo-Baroque style, executed by architects Alfred Lent, B. Scholz, and Gottlieb Henri Richard Lapierre, was intended to reflect the majesty and power of this revolutionary mode of travel. Like the Gare du Nord in Paris and London's Victoria Station, the Lehrte Station was not to be merely a shed to keep the rain off passengers as they waited for their train, it was to be a magnificent tribute to the power of steam.

As locomotive technology improved, trains leaving the Lehrte Station could reach distant cities in ever-shortening periods of time. In the 1920s, the Deutsche Reichsbahn boasted that passengers departing on the "Flying Hamburger" could reach the port city 179 miles away in just 2 1/4 hours. In terms of speed and price, this form of travel remained far superior to the airplane, and would continue to be so for decades to come.

With the collapse of the eastern front late in the war, the ruins of the Lehrte Station sheltered masses of refugees who had fled or been expelled from their homes in the Baltic territories, Poland and Czechoslo-vakia. By war's end, the homeless found themselves, like the rest of

*The Lehrte Station next to the River Spree in 1903.*
*In the background can be seen the regional Lehrte Station*
*(Lehrte S-Bahn Station)*

Berlin, encircled by the Red Army with all rail links severed and no chance to continue further west.

By October 1945, rail lines leading to Hanover were reopened, but travel was still restricted to the fortunate few who possessed proper documents. Even those with permission to leave the city had to stand in line for twelve hours before being issued a ticket.

The passenger trains that left Lehrte Station had to share the railway tracks with freight trains, many of which were packed with antiques and objets d'art. Most of these treasures had been sold by hungry Berliners to Allied officers and servicemen, primarily for cigarettes. In the months and years after the war, American cigarettes had replaced the reichsmark as the primary unit of exchange. The packs of cigarettes Berliners received for their heirlooms could be traded on the black markets around the Reichstag and the Potsdamer Platz for desperately needed food and supplies.

During these years of extreme hunger and privation, many relief trains arriving at the Lehrte Station from the West lost their contents to gangs of train robbers. Vital supplies were once again disrupted during the Russian blockade of the city in 1948.

The end of the war found the railway station in reasonably good shape, but its location in the British sector deep inside the GDR posed a problem. On August 28th, 1951, the rail line between West Berlin and Hamburg was closed down as part of the GDR's efforts to reduce access to

*View of the station looking*
*north-east in 1945*

West Berlin to a few tightly-controlled routes. Denied its raison d'être, the Lehrte Station was torn down six years later.

After the last of the rubble was cleared away, the railway terminus and its marshalling yards became a dumping ground for rusted equipment and construction material. The only remnant of the pre-war rail complex was the nearby regional (S-Bahn) railway station that dated back to 1882.

Construction of a resurrected Lehrte Station is now underway and will soon be ready to serve the thousands of government workers and visitors converging on the new group of federal buildings around the Spreebogen. Unfortunately, the old S-Bahn station is to be sacrificed to make way for the new project.

Following its projected completion date of 2004, the Lehrte Station will handle up to 30 million passengers per year and as such will become the busiest railhead in Europe. Design of the 430 metre-long main hall will follow the tradition of countless others like it. A network of glass panels anchored by high-tension cables will shelter the tracks and platforms and fill the area with natural light. Its architects, Gerkan, Marg and Partner have as their goal, "a renaissance of the railway station."

*Opposite: Refugees crowd the Lehrte Station during the mass exodus of displaced civilians from the east*

*Below: A forest of cranes help lay the foundations of the new Lehrte Station. When completed, it will be the largest railway terminus in Europe. In the background can be seen the Lehrte S-Bahn Station*

# APPENDIX

## Index

## Reading

**Akademie der Künste Berlin (ed.)** *Krieg – Zerstörung – Aufbau, Architektur und Stadtplanung 1940–1960, Berlin 1995*

**Balfour, Alan** *Berlin. The Politics of Order, New York 1990*

**Balfour, Alan (ed.)** *Berlin. World Cities, No 3, London 1995*

**Eckardt, Wolf von/Gilman, Sander L.** *Bertolt Brecht's Berlin, University of Nebraska 1993*

**Engel, Helmut** *Berlin auf dem Weg zur Moderne, Berlin 1997*

**Friedrich, Otto** *Before the Deluge, New York 1972*

**Gartendenkmalamt Berlin (ed.)** *Gartenkunst Berlin. 20 Jahre Gartendenkmalpflege in der Metropole, Berlin 1999*

**James, Kathleen** *Erich Mendelsohn and the Architecture of German Modernism, Cambridge University Press 1997*

**Kaes, Anton et al (ed.)** *The Weimar Republic Sourcebook, University of Chicago Press 1995*

**Kapitzki, Christel** *Neue Bahnhöfe in Berlin, Berlin 1998*

**Kuby, Erich** *The Russians and Berlin, Munich 1968*

**Ladd, Brian** *The Ghosts of Berlin. Confronting German History in the Urban Landscape, University of Chicago Press 1997*

**Le Tissier, Tony** *Berlin Then and Now, London 1992*

**MacDonough, Giles** *Berlin. A Portrait of Its History, Politics, Architecture, and Society, St. Martin's Press 1998*

Meyer, Ulf  *Bundeshauptstadt Berlin. Parlament, Regierung, Ländervertretungen, Botschaften, Berlin 1999*
Muhs, Andreas/Wefing, Heinrich  *Der Neue Potsdamer Platz. Ein Kunststück Stadt, Berlin 1998*
O'Donnell, James P.  *The Bunker, Boston 1978*
Pundt, Hermann  *Schinkel's Berlin, Harvard University Press 1972*
Reichardt, Hans J./Schäche, Wolfgang  *Von Berlin nach Germania. Über die Zerstörungen der Reichshauptstadt durch Albert Speers Neugestaltungsplanungen, Berlin 1998*
Richie, Alexandra  *Faust's Metropolis, New York 1998*

Rürup, Reinhard (ed.)  *Topographie des Terrors. Gestapo, SS und Reichssicherheitshauptamt auf dem "Prinz-Albrecht-Gelände", Berlin 1995*
Schäche, Wolfgang  *Architektur und Städtebau in Berlin zwischen 1933 und 1945, Berlin 1991*
Senatsverwaltung für Bau und Wohnungswesen (ed.)  *Hauptstadt Berlin. Zur Geschichte der Regierungsstandorte, Berlin 1992*
Senatsverwaltung für Stadtentwicklung und Umweltschutz (ed.)  *Hauptstadtplanung und Denkmalpflege. Die Standorte für Parlament und Regierung in Berlin, Berlin 1995*

Shirer, William  *Berlin Diary, Knopf 1941*
Staatliche Museen Berlin (Ost) (ed.)  *Karl Friedrich Schinkel 1781–1841, Berlin 1982*
Vassiltchikov, Marie  *Berlin Diaries 1940–1945, Vintage Books 1988*
Volk, Waltraud  *Berlin. Historische Strassen und Plätze heute, Berlin 1972*
Wilderotter, Hans  *Alltag der Macht. Berlin Wilhelmstrasse, Berlin 1998*
Wise, Michael Z.  *Capital Dilemma. Germany's Search for a New Architecture of Democracy, Princeton Architectural Press 1998*

## Photographic Acknowledgements

Architects Kollhoff and Timmermann, Berlin  p. 204
Architects Schweger + Partner, Hamburg  p. 140 (bottom)
Archiv Argon Verlag, Berlin  pp. 243, 249
Archiv für Kunst und Geschichte, Berlin  pp. 21 (top), 50 (2, top), 92 (top), 99, 103, 104/105 (2), 107 (top), 139 (top), 149 (top), 202, 232
Bettmann Archives (CORBIS), London/Picture Press, Hamburg  pp. 64/65, 76 (right), 252
Bildarchiv Preussischer Kulturbesitz, Berlin  pp. 4/5, 8/9, 10, 12 (left), 17 (bottom, Friedrich Seidenstücker [F. S.]), 20 (F. Albert Schwartz [F. A. S.]), 25 (top), 28 (Emil Leitner), 35 (top left) (Hoffmann), 58 (left), 58 (right, Oskar Dahlke), 59 (bottom, F. S.), 60 (F. S.), 65 (right), 70 (F. S.), 72, 73 (F. A. S.), 74 (Herbert Hensky), 86 (Heinrich Hoffmann), 87 (top right), 89 (Benno Wundshammer), 92 (bottom), 94, 97 (left), 102 (top left, Stöcker), 102 (top right, Hanns Hubmann), 108 (bottom, Arthur Grimm), 112/113, 116 (F. S.), 132 (left), 132 (right, Felix H. Man), 136 (right), 143 (right), 144 (left, Franz Kräft), 152 (left, F. S.), 154 (bottom left), 162 (right, Carl Weinrother), 164 (top), 176 (left), 182 (left), 183, 190 (Georg Ebert), 195 (top), 206 (right), 207 (top), 212, 213, 216 (right), 220 (2, Emil Leitner), 223, 226, 238 (F. S.), 242
Canadian Centre for Architecture, Montreal  pp. 32 (2), 33, 155 (top)

Deutsches Historisches Museum, Berlin  pp. 14, 21 (bottom), 82, 83, 84, 137, 140 (top), 188 (right), 236 (bottom)
Mark R. McGee, Montreal  pp. 16, 22 (2), 35 (top right), 40 (top), 46 (bottom right), 66, 87 (bottom), 124, 136 (left), 160 (right), 168, 170/171, 173, 184 (right), 188 (left), 207 (bottom), 216 (left), 239 (top)
Landesarchiv Berlin  pp. 36, 78 (bottom left), 91 (left), 95, 114 (2), 138/139 (bottom), 148/149 (bottom), 154 (bottom right), 160 (left), 162 (left), 165, 176 (right), 179 (bottom), 184 (left), 194, 199, 208/209, 219 (top)
Landesbildstelle Berlin  pp. 12 (right), 13, 31 (top), 42/43, 45 (top), 46 (top left), 47, 52, 53, 56 (3), 59 (top), 62/63, 68, 87 (top left), 88 (2), 109 (2), 115 (top), 117 (2), 120/121, 122/123, 126/127, 128 (top), 128/129, 133 (bottom), 142, 143 (left), 144/145, 155 (bottom), 161, 164 (bottom), 167, 172 (2), 185 (2), 189, 198 (right), 200, 201, 214 (top), 217, 221, 227 (2), 231 (top, middle), 246
Jonas Maron, Berlin  pp. 15 (bottom), 18/19, 23, 27, 31 (bottom), 35 (bottom), 41, 45 (bottom), 50 (bottom), 51, 57, 61, 67, 71 (bottom), 75, 80/81, 85, 93, 97 (right), 101, 106/107 (bottom), 111, 115 (bottom), 118/119, 125, 131, 135, 141, 147, 152/153, 159, 163 (bottom), 169, 174/175, 180/181, 182 (right), 186/187, 191 (bottom), 195 (bottom), 197, 205,

211, 215, 219 (bottom), 225, 229, 231 (bottom), 237 (bottom), 241 (bottom), 247, 253
Museum Berlin Karlshorst  pp. 15 (top), 34, 48, 236 (top), 250/251
National Archives, Washington DC  pp. 17 (top), 24 (2), 25 (bottom), 37, 38/39 (2), 49 (right), 54/55, 71 (middle), 77, 78 (top left), 78/79, 90, 91 (right), 96, 98, 108 (top), 133 (top), 150/151, 156 (left), 156/157, 163 (top), 179 (top), 193, 222, 240, 241 (top), 244/245
Stiftung Stadtmuseum Berlin  pp. 69, 71 (top), 76 (left), 102 (bottom), 126 (left), 177, 191 (top), 198 (left), 206 (left, Hermann Rückwardt), 214 (bottom), 235, 237 (top), 239 (bottom)
Ullstein Bilderdienst, Berlin  pp. 29 (left, Hanns Hubmann), 29 (right), 30 (top, Arthur v. Brietzke), 120 (left, H. v. Perkhammer)
U.S. Embassy Public Affairs, Berlin  p. 30 (bottom)
Wolfgang Volz/Bilderberg, Christo and Jeanne-Claude, Wrapped Reichstag, Berlin 1971–1995  p. 40 (bottom)

Jacket photographs
Front: Landesbildstelle Berlin (top), Museum Berlin Karlshorst (middle), Jonas Maron, Berlin (bottom)
Spine: Jonas Maron, Berlin
Back: National Archives, Washington DC